EAT LIKE

it matters

EAT LIKE

it matters

· · · · · · ·

HOW I LOST 120 POUNDS AND FOUND MY
INNER BADASS (AND HOW YOU CAN TOO!)

MARILYN MCKENNA

Published by Seismic Shift LLC, Bellevue, Washington
http://itmattersmag.com

Edited and Designed by Girl Friday Productions
www.girlfridayproductions.com
Editorial: Gail Hudson
Design: Paul Barrett
Cover photograph: © Kate Baldwin Photography
Food and Prop Styling: Malina Lopez

ISBN-13: 9780692472606
ISBN-10: 0692472606
e-ISBN: 9780692472613

First Edition

Printed in the United States of America

For my husband, Rob.
Your sunny optimism is my guiding light.

Contents

● ● ● ● ● ● ●

Introduction

······

I 've had more than one person tell me that writing a weight-loss book is a crazy idea. Fortunately, those people are very good friends, so I didn't take it too personally. Truth be told, though, they're probably right. It's not that these friends don't think my 120-pound weight loss is inspiring; they applaud my having kept it off for more than eight years. It's just that . . . well, you've seen the diet sections of bookstores! They practically have to shore up the shelves to keep them from collapsing under the weight of all of those books. There are already thousands of books that have been written about weight loss. It's hard to imagine that anything remains unsaid about the subject.

WE'RE NOT IN KANSAS ANYMORE
(OR HOW THIS BOOK IS DIFFERENT FROM EVERY DIET BOOK YOU'VE EVER READ)

But I believe there is room for my perspective. In fact, I think my perspective is absolutely vital. Few of those weight-loss books were written by people who have been obese and then lost weight. Most of them were written by doctors, nutritionists, or personal trainers. I won't dispute their good intentions, and they certainly have lots of letters after their names. Some of those authors are famous, and you might pick up their book because you've heard of them or seen them on TV. But do they really understand the struggles of someone who is over-weight or obese? Is there a difference between taking advice from someone who has studied obesity and understands how it works on an academic level, and someone who has lived it and eventually overcome it? Obviously, I do think there's a sig-nificant difference.

Until eight years ago I was fat. (I apologize if that word offends you; I don't use it to describe anyone but myself.) In fact, I had been fat for most of my life—from the time I was seven years old until I was forty-four. There were a few years during my late teens and early twenties during which I starved myself into a normal-looking body, but there was absolutely nothing normal about what was going on inside my head. If a dog year equals seven human years, then a "fat year" equals an eternity. Which means I was fat for a very long time. During that time I read more of those diet books than your great-aunt Wilma has Precious Moments figurines. So yeah, I read a lot of them.

The best of them offer scientific research and/or medical explanations for why we overeat and what happens inside our bodies when we do. A few of these high-quality books have given me a great deal of insight into my own food triggers and why some foods seem to stomp all over my free will until the cravings take on a life of their own. The worst of these books offer up platitudes and clichés that we've all heard a thousand times before. It isn't necessarily that they're wrong, but what overweight or obese person doesn't already know that they should remove the skin from chicken before they eat it? Not only do we know that, but most of us are dieting experts. We can tell you that brown rice has more fiber than white rice, that we should chew slowly and eat without distractions, and that kale is the new "it" vegetable. But what good is knowing any of that if we're still driven to eat Cheez-Its out of the box at ten o'clock at night?

Obesity and being overweight aren't intellectual problems. Nor do they occur in a vacuum; they happen in the context of families. Whether it's our family of origin, the family we've created as adults, or some combination of the two, each family has its own food culture within the context of our broader culture. We learn our eating habits, declare our preferences, and even pick up a few food neuroses within our families.

THERE IS A DIFFERENCE BETWEEN TAKING WEIGHT LOSS ADVICE FROM SOMEONE WHO UNDERSTANDS IT ACADEMICALLY AND SOMEONE WHO'S LIVED IT.

My own story is no different. As you'll read, I was a fat kid before childhood obesity was on our national radar. I was raised on Hostess Ding Dongs and Ho Hos, and Cap'n Crunch cereal (Peanut Butter Crunch for me, Crunch Berries for my brother). And yet I was admonished for eating too much. "Maybe someday you'll care about how you look and you won't eat that," I was told. I'd watch excitedly as my mother baked pies, cookies, cakes, and other sweets and wait eagerly to eat the raw scraps of dough and lick the mixer's beater; then I was dropped off at a Weight Watchers meeting, alone, because I was "too fat."

As a young teen I had a stepfather who kept a strict accounting of how many potato chips were in the bag; any discrepancy between what was "supposed" to be there and what was actually there meant hours of humiliating verbal attacks directed at me. When confronted with these accusations, I would either say I fed the food to the dog—better to be thought of as stupid than gluttonous—or I would simply shut down. Somewhere deep inside I believe that my empathy for others who are suffering stems from this trauma. I was ill equipped to defend myself as a child; the helplessness and shame I felt stayed with me into adulthood, long after my mom divorced my stepfather a few years later. The fact that I can still put myself in that vulnerable little girl's head so easily speaks volumes of the devastating blow this type of emotional abuse can deal to a child's fragile self-esteem.

I offer these examples only as a point of reference. My experiences shaped me and some of my difficulties with food, but I've certainly heard far worse from others. We all carry emotional baggage from our childhood into adulthood; for some those bags are heavier than they are for others. My own experiences taught me that it's possible to inflict a great deal of damage on a child's psyche—damage that may take a very long time to repair. It is because of my childhood experiences and my own failings as a parent (which you'll read about in chapter eleven) that I know we need to step up and do better by our children. I believe it's possible to break the cycle of emotional eating within one generation, and I'm working hard to achieve that within my own family. Imagine what an incredible gift this is to our children.

Even though this book will undoubtedly end up on those overstuffed shelves at the bookstore—along with all the other diet books—it is not a diet book. It's a story about how I hit rock bottom—with my weight but also with a lot of other issues that made me feel like a failure. It's also a story about how different the world looked from that very dark place and how the decisions I made there shaped my transformation. And while you will find a handful of my favorite go-to recipes here, you won't find specific meal plans or grocery shopping lists. I've read dozens—hundreds, probably—of books that contain those weight-loss staples, and not one of them ever helped me lose a single pound.

SUCCESS COMES FROM FINDING THE COURAGE WITHIN TO WANT SOMETHING BETTER FOR YOURSELF AND HAVING THE GUTS TO GO AFTER IT WITH EVERYTHING YOU'VE GOT.

What I know for sure is that weight loss doesn't work by trying to re-create somebody else's success. Success comes from finding the courage within to want something better for yourself and having the guts to go after it with everything you've got.

I offer up my own experience only as a reference—or maybe a starting point—for your own transformation. What I hope to show is that I was right there with you, lost in all the hopelessness and desperation that obesity can bring. And yet somehow, amid all that despair, I found the will to change. It has been a metamorphosis of my body certainly, but the physical change is permanent because I have also completely overhauled how I view myself, how I express myself, what I want for myself, and what I'm willing to do to get it.

As much as I hope my personal journey is interesting and even inspiring to you, I also hope that you will tap into that same tenacity and drive to propel your own transformation. Whatever that source of strength is for you—and it is as individualized as your fingerprint—you'll never find it poring over diet books and meal plans.

What you'll find in these pages is a compassionate ear and an unqualified belief that you too are capable of transforming your body and your life, just like I did. And just like me, you'll realize that you've had the power within you all along to transform yourself. As we walk this path together, I'll ask you to

---

TO CLAIM THE SUCCESS WE MUST OWN THE SOLUTION.

---

unflinchingly look at yourself and be open to thinking about weight loss in a whole new way. If you're willing to kick your excuses and the status quo to the curb and look honestly at your own habits and behaviors, you will discover what it really takes to lose weight and keep it off for the rest of your life.

The ultimate truth of healthy living is that nobody can do this for us: there is no magic diet pill, no miracle diet, no sweeping government program. And even though I'm a sucker for a schmaltzy rom com, no knight in shining armor is gonna come to our rescue either. It's gonna take grit, determination, and courage—and a whole lotta sweat. (Because in the twenty-first century, our story's heroine has a spin class she's gotta get to after work.)

To claim the success we must own the solution.

This is a personal journey: yours and mine. Along the way we'll challenge mainstream assumptions about weight loss and healthy living, we'll share practical advice and daily changes we can implement today to start feeling better right away, and we'll talk about the nuts and bolts of maintaining a healthy lifestyle for the long haul.

I don't know about you, but I've had more than enough of preachy "diet experts" who don't really know what it's like to be overweight or obese.

Instead I offer my no-holds-barred real-world story of how I changed from a morbidly obese, miserable woman to a fit and healthy, embarrassingly happy woman. In the chapters that follow, I'll talk specifically about how I overhauled my eating habits, changing them from out of control to disciplined and purposeful. I'll show how I evolved from couch potato to marathon runner by finding joy in moving my body. I'll discuss what it really means to just say no to the sometimes oppressive demands that infringe on our time, and I'll describe how I learned to prioritize my own health and wellness without the guilt that often tells us that putting our own needs first is selfish. And maybe most revealingly of all, I'll talk about the reasons I failed to lose weight during the twenty-plus years that I bounced from diet to diet and share how I finally found success on my terms.

What I think you'll find in this book is so much more than just the story of how I harnessed my own potential: it's about how you can achieve yours too. We all deserve our own happily ever after. We all deserve to be the hero or heroine in our own story. There is no dress rehearsal for life; the curtain is going up and it's time to take our place center stage.

Chapter One

MAYBE YOU CAN'T BREAK THROUGH UNTIL YOU ADMIT YOU'RE BROKEN

I once weighed 265 pounds and had a body mass index of 43. To clarify, the National Institutes of Health labels as "overweight" those people with a body mass index (BMI) of between 25 and 29.9. Those who have a BMI of between 30 and 39.9 are considered to be "obese," and those with a BMI of 40 and above are classified as having "clinically severe obesity." I was, by medical definition, what is more commonly labeled morbidly obese. I now weigh 145 pounds and my BMI is 23, which is smack-dab in the middle of the "normal" range. Considering the drastic change, it's no surprise that people ask me all the time how I did it. I can see the longing in their eyes, a desperation that I too once felt.

Some people just want a quickie five-word answer ("I did the _____ Diet"), but others actually want the whole story.

They want to know how I transformed myself from someone who had been morbidly obese for decades into a marathon runner who enjoys a vigorous, active lifestyle and preaches healthy living to anyone within a fifty-foot radius. Even more, they want to know how they can channel some of that mojo for themselves. They want their own body makeover, and they hope I can help them figure out how to do it. This book is my answer to these questions: How do I transform my body? How can I improve my health?

A transformation as dramatic as mine suggests visions of a grand epiphany: the heavens open up and beams of glorious light shine down. People imagine that the lucky recipient of this euphoric enlightenment is filled with a wellspring of self-awareness and suddenly evolves into a more perfect version of herself. She magically transforms from a fat, slovenly failure into someone who always wants to eat right and goes to the gym. Always motivated, always on top of her game, the subject of this divine conversion is the picture of health and happiness forevermore with nary a care in the world.

Hmmmm, maybe that's what weight loss looks like for some people, but my own conversion was somewhat less than awe inspiring.

After a life spent as a fat kid, then as a manic diet-crazed teen, and finally as a morbidly obese adult, by the time I'd reached my forties I no longer dreamed of such glorious revelation. In fact, my own life-changing turning point was less Hollywood cinematic splendor and more hitting rock bottom and realizing there was nowhere to go but up.

ABJECT MISERY

In the spring of 2007 I was an overwhelmed full-time working mom, with four active kids between the ages of seven and nineteen and a husband who was the attorney general of Washington State. To say we were stretched thin would be a gross understatement. Our days moved at lightning speed; our evenings were at full throttle. Weekends were no better. My girls, at nineteen and sixteen, were launching into young adulthood. My boys were eleven and seven at the time, both active in school, Scouts, and various sports, depending on the season. The minivan was perpetually running on empty, and so was I. On weeknights I'd dash in the door at 6:00 p.m. after working a full day, throw dinner together in order to get all the kids fed by 6:15, and race out to whatever evening activity we had planned. Saturdays there were back-to-back soccer games, and during them I'd find myself asleep in a folding chair while I was supposed to be cheering my boys on. My husband was plugged into our lives but completely absorbed in managing his offices, traveling around the state and country, and planning another statewide reelection campaign for the coming year. It was difficult, if not impossible, for him to be hands on at home.

Back on the front lines, I was in a state of near-constant panic. I was getting things done as best I could, but not doing anything well. There was no way to prioritize which tasks were most important because there were so many in front of me that were absolute emergencies, and I only had time to deal with those. Everything was urgent. Everything should have been dealt with yesterday. There was no planning—hell, there was no *thinking*! There was only the never-ending demand for doing.

I recall one day sharing with a coworker my frustration at trying to balance these countless demands, and she suggested

I make a list of all the household tasks that needed to be done and who was doing each. Once I had a list, she calmly advised, I could begin prioritizing and delegating. Aha! Division of labor! That seemed like a brilliant solution, so I set about making a list. Four single-spaced pages into a list of tasks that were mine alone, I stopped. It was too depressing. I felt completely hopeless about making a dent in the problem. My husband wasn't going to get less busy. In fact, I knew that he would only continue to get *busier* as we ramped up to his 2008 campaign. My kids were trying to help, but I was manning the ship. I was the captain.

And I was going down.

On top of this strain, I was more than one hundred pounds overweight. I had been overweight as a child, and starved myself thin as a teenager and in my early twenties, only to start gaining weight as soon as the ink was dry on my marriage license. It wasn't a conscious decision, of course. It's just that I was fully embracing my role as wife and homemaker: wanting to cook the perfect meals, host the perfect gatherings for our families, and be the perfect hostess for Rob's colleagues in his burgeoning career. It didn't help my waistline that I became pregnant before our first anniversary. It was certainly no longer required for women to define themselves solely as wives and mothers when Rob and I married in the mid-1980s, but I latched onto these roles with all my might. I'd had an unconventional, nomadic childhood and longed for a sense of stability. I embraced traditionalism with the zeal of an anarchist.

Pregnancy, not surprisingly, brought weight gain. I put on roughly fifty pounds with my first child, though she weighed only about seven pounds at birth. I went back to work eight weeks later and hung on to a good number of the remaining forty-three pounds. Fast-forward three years and I had another little girl and gained another fifty pounds. She weighed eight pounds. Woo-hoo! Only an extra forty-two pounds this time!

As every parent knows, the duties and responsibilities of parenthood grow exponentially with each child. By the time the second one comes along there is no time to follow that sage advice to "sleep when the baby sleeps." Numbers three and four mean you're nursing in the grocery store and doing laundry at 3:00 a.m. Whether you have children or not, you probably know that being exhausted and overextended for a long period of time takes a huge physical and mental toll.

That toll was magnified by the fact that waaaaaaaay back at the onset of my life as a mom, I decided that I couldn't leave my young children in someone else's care. I berated myself for putting my first child in day care, thinking, *Kids get sick all the time in day care, and it's horribly expensive,* and I felt guilty as hell, so when my second child came along I started my own day care in our home. For nearly a decade I ran a state-licensed in-home day care—caring for my four children plus many more—for upwards of sixty hours a week.

I hated it. I don't just mean I disliked it. I really *hated* it.

I hated nearly everything about that life: the complete lack of freedom, the absence of personal goals or any sense of accomplishment, the isolation. When I look back on those years from where I sit now, I am shocked that the only lasting negative consequence of my misery was that I became obese. I persevered for as long as I did because we desperately needed the money. I carried on, but my misery fed a torrent of negative emotions: I resented my husband and my older children's freedom, I was angry that we were so financially strapped that I had no alternatives, and I was jealous of other families who seemed to have a more balanced workload. I felt trapped, yet I was resigned to a kind of martyr mentality that changed me into someone who was bitter, sarcastic, passive-aggressive, and desperately unhappy.

My own kids had friends over for playdates, as most children do, and I remember an instance when one of their little friends looked up at me after I tied his shoes so he could go out and play; I heaved an exasperated, put-upon sigh, and he said, "Why are you so angry?" I still hear that innocent seven-year-old voice all these years later. Why indeed?

Like many of you, I wasn't just busy with family and work; I volunteered in many of the organizations that were a part of my world. I was the neighborhood homeowners' association president, a PTA executive board member, Sunday school teacher, church choir member . . . and on and on. Of course, these are all valuable activities, but in many respects I participated out of obligation and a need to prove that I was a supportive wife, a devoted mother, a devout churchgoer, and a dedicated community member. I never asked myself if I found any intrinsic pleasure in these tasks; I did them because I desperately needed the validation that doing them brought me.

BEING THE GOOD WIFE IN THE POLITICAL LIMELIGHT

All of this was really going on in the background of my life, though. From the time our oldest children were very young, my husband was a full-time elected official—first elected to the Metropolitan King County Council (in Seattle) in 1995—and I was a politician's wife. The pressure to be the perfect wife is immense if you want your husband to be successful in politics, which, of course, I did. Rob is smart, energetic, driven, and can roll up his sleeves and get into the nitty-gritty policy issues of government like nobody's business. Plus, political life was what he wanted, so I wanted it for him. He was elected, then reelected two more times, serving a total of nine years on our county's legislative council. Over those years he made a name for himself as someone who was pragmatic, well liked, and—very important—electable.

In 2003 the sitting attorney general ran for governor, which meant her former office was open. As a lawyer and well-respected elected official, Rob was at the top of everyone's short list to run for attorney general. When he stepped onto the stage of a statewide campaign, so did our entire family. This was a level of pressure and scrutiny none of us had experienced before. The time and energy this kind of undertaking demands is hard to describe to those who have never been on the inside of a statewide political campaign. All other concerns are pushed aside; all complaints seem trivial because the goal is paramount. It is essentially a marathon done at a 5K pace; that is, an all-out effort over a very long period of time with no rest.

Naturally, he won because he was the superior candidate and he's a superstar. (I may be ever-so-slightly biased.) Our lives became public in a way we had never experienced before. The demands on Rob's time escalated enormously—truly, he has the broadest bandwidth of any human being I know. This frenetic, very public life became our "normal" for the next eight years.

Rob's becoming attorney general brought with it enough of a financial cushion that I could stop running the day care. I still needed to work, but I had an opportunity to go back to school for a short time and get a paralegal certificate so that I could work outside the home again, which I hadn't done since our second child was born. I did so, and within a couple of years I was that crazed woman you met at the beginning of this story: the overwhelmed full-time working mom, with four

15

active kids and a workaholic husband who was attorney general of Washington State.

So how did my weight play into all of this?

ONE REALLY BAD DAY

Being a politician's wife is all about appearances. You are prominent but not substantive. You are essential but not relevant. You can do great harm if you're a liability in some way: too loud, too opinionated, too high maintenance. You are to be supportive, adoring, and servile. It's an anachronistic role that I hope will modernize eventually, but while we were in the thick of things, this was very much expected. And by all outward measures, I was very good at it.

From the outside, I appeared to have a charmed life, a *Leave It to Beaver* existence that seemed perfect in every way: adoring husband, beautiful children, lovely home. But I felt like a fraud. Inside I was a wreck, a mass of anxiety and worry. As a political spouse you're thrust into the limelight as a sort of default running mate. Yet there I was, this morbidly obese woman, standing next to my handsome, successful, rising-star husband feeling like a complete and utter impostor. In my head I thought, *They're all looking at me. There is nowhere to hide! They can all see how fat I am. How out of control I am. They're wondering what he's even doing with me.*

Smile and wave, smile and wave.

Though my husband's supporters have always been incredibly gracious to me, I had the sense that it wasn't really me they saw. They cast me in the same glowing light in which they saw him, but I felt I'd done nothing to deserve such esteem. I was merely the person standing next to him. Proximity to greatness isn't greatness. Though I was convinced I had done nothing to deserve praise, and was worried that both my brash personality and my obesity would reflect badly on Rob, I vowed that I would do everything in my power to be the consummate political wife.

So I performed on cue: smile and wave, smile and wave.

The high-stakes public scrutiny of being Rob's wife, on top of an already stressful home and work life, sent me reeling. I was coping, just barely, by stuffing down all of that anger, resentment, fear, anxiety, insecurity, and angst with food.

The human psyche is a fascinating thing. Under stress some of us lash out, some drink ourselves into oblivion, and many do what I did: eat. It's a conditioned response, of course, one that I learned in childhood. Food is comforting and a socially acceptable coping mechanism. The staggering number of overweight and obese Americans—69 percent of adults aged twenty and older, according to the US Centers for Disease Control and Prevention—leads me to believe that my experience isn't an anomaly.

At the political and public events I attended with Rob, and even at home with my own family, I ate sensibly. I cooked typical American family-friendly meals at home—meatloaf, spaghetti and meatballs . . . Taco Tuesday, anyone? Going out was always a treat, but often meant a set menu at a hotel dining room where portion sizes were huge, or making dinner out of hors d'oeuvres at a political fundraiser. Exactly how many calories are in a tray of Brie and crackers? I dunno, but if each calorie earned you a frequent-flyer mile, I probably could have flown to France and back, free of charge.

In private, I ate in a frenzied way that only those of us who know this demon can understand. When I was alone, I wasn't judged. I could be myself. I could relax. Eating calmed me down. I wouldn't necessarily say it made me happy, but it made my unhappiness bearable. My manic binge eating when I was alone was how I coped with the stress of my circumstances, which felt impossible to change. My feelings of helplessness had no voice; I dared not let myself become truly conscious of these thoughts because then I would be forced to confront them.

Further complicating the situation was the fact that my husband is the quintessential bright-eyed optimist. He couldn't really understand my worries, doubts, and fears. Rob just doesn't think that way, so he didn't make allowances for the possibility that I didn't share his sunny outlook. In our rare conversations about why I was unhappy, he would tell me that we just had to redouble our efforts and try harder to keep things in balance. We lived in a constant state of financial stress, so the pressure I felt to bring in more money while simultaneously reducing our expenses was an oppressive force in our lives. I bore the weight of this strain by constantly lowering my own expectations of what I felt I could hope for. I stopped getting my hair done at a salon. I stopped going out with friends. Eventually, I stopped hoping for anything to get better. Meanwhile Rob's view was that better times were just ahead if we could only see past our short-term circumstances. Though his cheerfulness was intended to be reassuring, it felt dismissive. What I heard was that I was miserable because I wasn't trying hard enough, or because I lacked the vision to see beyond my current situation.

And yet my troubles were real, and by the spring of 2007 I was hanging on by a thread. One day that spring, amid the chaos of my home life, my feelings of hopelessness, and the loneliness I felt in my marriage, I was called into my boss's office for a performance review.

Mother. Of. God.

I was terrified.

At the time, I was working as a paralegal at a high-end Seattle family law firm. I'd been there less than a year and was still on the steep side of the learning curve. Though I'd gone back to school to get a paralegal certificate, there's a good deal that must be learned on the job. My bosses and I sat down to

I WOULDN'T NECESSARILY SAY EATING MADE ME HAPPY, BUT IT MADE MY UNHAPPINESS BEARABLE.

discuss some of the tasks I performed well: I was friendly, personable, and professional, they said. Everyone liked me and felt I was a good fit for the office. I learned quickly and could multitask efficiently. *This is good!* I thought. *It's a crazy, hard job, but I'm doing well! I've made a few mistakes, but I learned from them, and I'm holding my own.* Then the hammer fell. In addition to my aforementioned good traits, I was disorganized, I procrastinated, and I talked to my kids on the phone too often.

Have I mentioned I don't take criticism well? Not even constructive, well-intentioned criticism. I tried to talk but no sound came out. I was horrified. I wasn't doing a good job? I was failing? Pain and shame washed over me, and I crumbled. When I tried to respond, all that came out was that squeaky four-year-old voice that happens when you're trying desperately not to cry but you know it's inevitable. In fact, within seconds I was bawling.

Had I not been in such an emotionally fragile state I probably would have dealt with the situation differently. Had I not been strained to the breaking point, I might not have sobbed uncontrollably and blurted out, "I can't do this anymore! I quit!"

But that's what happened.

Once I dried my tears and headed home that evening, it really began to hit me: I had just quit my job. Completely impulsively, without discussing it with Rob. And on top of everything else, I was lumbering through life in a body that brought me nothing but shame. I felt like a failure on the inside, and it seemed that my weight was the outward manifestation of my failure for everyone to see and judge. And though I was trying as hard as I possibly could to be everything I thought I should be, I was losing the battle.

If I could go back in time and whisper something in my own ear at that moment when I was confronted with my failings at work, feeling the full weight of my inability to be the perfect wife and mother and the disgust I felt about my body and my manic overeating—that moment when my whole world seemed to come crashing down around me—I think I would simply tell myself, *Just sit down for a moment, dear, and breathe.*

Instead, I quit my job and headed home to face my husband, who I knew would be absolutely livid about what I'd just done.

Yes, it was a really bad day.

Rather than two ships passing in the night, I would describe my relationship with Rob during this time as two Japanese bullet trains passing on parallel tracks. Our conversations centered on logistics: who was coming, who was going, how much money was in the checking account, and scheduling. Always scheduling. But on my way home from work that day I knew I had to tell him what I'd done. He was home that night by some miracle, so after dinner I suggested we take a walk at the high school track across the street from our house. As we walked, I started to tell him that I'd impulsively quit my job—a job that represented one-third of our much-needed income—and I turned back into that four-year-old girl whose squeaky voice could barely utter the words. I attempted to convey my misery and my desperation, but it came out a muddled mess.

Rob doesn't really get mad; Rob gets quiet. In this case, he got really, really quiet. My admission was not met with an outpouring of sympathy. My husband is an overachiever of the highest order; he just assumes that everyone thrives on the same kind of hyperscheduled, superdemanding level of activity that he's mastered. He is also not a man who likes surprises, especially when it comes to our financial life.

"We need the money," he scolded. "What are we going to do about that? We're on the cusp of paying for college tuition—for which we've saved almost nothing!"

I didn't have an answer for him in that moment. He was completely right, of course, which just made me feel worse. How could I explain that I couldn't do it all? The final nail in the coffin was my body itself, which disgusted me. It represented everything I had failed at. I don't know if there is an emotion deeper than misery, but if there is, that's what I felt.

OPRAH HAS "AHA!" MOMENTS; I HAVE "OH SHIT!" MOMENTS

When I talk to people about this experience now, I describe it as a sort of perfect storm of life circumstances, or as my rock bottom. Whatever the metaphor, there was certainly a feeling of, *"Oh shit! Now what?"*

The days that followed that really bad day were difficult, to be sure. I felt lost and confused. I was humiliated by my failure, but unlike previous times I'd failed at something in my

life (most often dieting), my humiliation didn't give way to resignation as it had always done before. This time it gave way to
surrender. I had tried so hard to succeed at the roles I played—
politician's wife, attentive mother, diligent worker, engaged
volunteer—*and yet I had still failed.* If you're trying as hard
as you possibly can at something and you still fail—you have
no choice but to stop and ask yourself some questions. Those
questions kept interrupting my thoughts as I frantically sent
out résumés to find another job. In between phone calls and
e-mails, my mind kept circling back to these same questions:
*What would happen if I just stopped trying to be all of those
things to all of those people? What if I tried defining happiness
and success for myself? What would that look like?*

The very first thing that popped into my head was not
something I would do, but rather something I wouldn't do. I
would not spend the rest of my life fat and miserable, stuffing
down my feelings and substituting someone else's definition of
success for my own.

In my despair, everything seemed to be in shambles: my
work, my home life, my marriage, my self-esteem. As out of
control as my weight was, it suddenly seemed like the most
manageable problem on the table. It also seemed to be ground
zero for so many of the other issues that plagued me. I would
realize later that my weight was both the manifestation and the
source of much of my unhappiness. At the time all I knew was
that so many other things felt completely beyond my control,
but I felt I could take control of this. It seemed like the best—
and only—place where I could start putting everything back
together again.

Surrendering the expectation that I could be all things to
all people stemmed from a deep realization that I had personal
worth. Simply put, it was a spiritual and emotional acknowledgment that I deserved happiness, that my life had purpose

and meaning beyond my current circumstances. I have always had self-esteem issues, but at that moment, somewhere in the core of my being, I knew that I was worth fixing. Of course, finally realizing this and actually taking action are two different things entirely. I knew that I had to seize this moment, as dark and desperate as it was, to change myself.

LAP-BAND SURGERY

About six months before my life imploded, I'd asked my family doctor about weight-loss surgery, specifically the laparoscopic gastric banding (lap-band) procedure. I'd done some research and learned that the lap-band is the only type of weight-loss surgery that is entirely reversible. It wouldn't remove or rearrange my internal organs, or impede my ability to digest nutrients from the food I ate. It also has a much lower surgical risk than other types of weight-loss surgery—in particular the popular gastric bypass surgery, a procedure that removes most of the stomach and small intestine. I understand that gastric bypass is a lifesaving surgery for some, but the lengthy, complex surgery made me nervous, and I like my stomach and colon whole and right where they are, thanks very much. I tentatively asked my doctor if the lap-band might be a viable option for me.

Alas, her reaction was discouraging. In her very doctorly way she dismissed the idea outright, saying that the surgery hadn't been around long enough to have adequate long-range data on its effectiveness or safety. "It's not a good idea to have a foreign object in your body like that unless you absolutely need to, like a pacemaker or something." And her parting words, which I'd heard a thousand times before but which this time felt especially condescending and indifferent: "You really just need to make better food choices and exercise more."

23

Gee, thanks. I never thought of that.

Trust me, there isn't one overweight person on the face of the earth who hasn't thought of that. Obesity isn't an intellectual problem. Fat people aren't fat because they're stupid. If they're like me, they're fat because they're using food as a coping mechanism to deal with very complicated emotional issues. My doctor's dismissal felt like a slap in the face. But I assumed because of her vastly superior medical knowledge that she must be right. I was deflated as the door to another possible solution slammed shut in my face.

Fast-forward six months to my moment of crisis. I'd seen no improvement in my physical health in the intervening months between my doctor's dismissive rejection of weight-loss surgery and my collapse. In fact, I was fatter than ever. Having decided that my weight was at the vortex of the issues that led to my undoing, I knew that this was where I had to focus my energy. I also knew—from decades of failed diets—that I was done with things that didn't work.

Despite my doctor's warning against lap-band surgery, I called a surgical center and set up an appointment. Once there, I met with a psychologist who evaluated me, went through my entire physical history with a nurse, and finally met one of the surgeons. Intuitively, the procedure made sense to me, which was comforting. I understood the mechanics of the device, and I believed I could commit to the required eating and lifestyle changes. I was also a good candidate for surgery from a medical standpoint. One small problem: my insurance wouldn't cover it and the cost was a stratospheric $18,000.

Gasp! Wheeze! Choke! These were the imagined sounds of my husband coughing up a lung when I told him the price.

I forged ahead anyway. "I've decided to have lap-band surgery," I told Rob one evening when I'd finally worked up the nerve. "I've discussed it with a surgeon, and I feel like it's the right solution for me. It's expensive, but I've worked out how we can pay for it. I really need your support on this."

To his everlasting credit, my long-suffering husband did not cough up a lung, and, in fact, he supported my decision. I think he could tell how resolute I was, how much I needed

OBESITY ISN'T AN INTELLECTUAL PROBLEM.

the change, considering the downward spiral I'd been in for so long, and, most important, how committed I was to making this work and changing my life. We were in it together.

The decision to undergo lap-band surgery was life changing in many ways. For starters, the money for the surgery was no small sacrifice for our family of six. I'd scaled back my job (I found another paralegal job that was closer to home, and I was working only four days a week while making considerably less money), our eldest daughter was a freshman in college, and we were staring down a couple of decades' worth of higher-education tuition payments for her and for our three younger children.

In addition to the financial sacrifice, I had some serious emotional baggage to work through. I was deeply aware that many people consider weight-loss surgery a gimmick or a way of cheating at weight loss. In fact, I was so fearful of being judged that I kept my decision to have surgery a secret from everyone other than my immediate family. I didn't even tell my closest friends for over a year.

I've since come to terms with it, but I confess it still bothers me when I hear people refer to weight-loss surgery as "an easy way out." Ha! Wrong! The lap-band is a tool, much like using a personal trainer is a tool for getting in shape. A trainer can help devise a plan for you, can encourage you, can provide expertise and accountability, but you're the one on the ground doing the push-ups. Likewise, the lap-band can't make you eat right.

There exists a strange relationship between weight and virtue in our culture that we don't apply to other personal behaviors. We don't think people who use nicotine patches to quit smoking, for example, are cheating simply because they didn't go cold turkey. We support people doing whatever they need to get over addictions like gambling, drugs, and alcohol, but when it comes to food, we fret over whether someone does it the "right" way.

There's so much judgment in our assessment of why people are overweight or obese, and there is equally as much judgment regarding how people choose to combat it. But to those who would dismiss weight-loss surgery as a "cheat," may I suggest that it is no panacea. By some estimates, over 60 percent of people who have weight-loss surgery "fail" at it by gaining back some or all of the weight they initially lose. Rather than seeing the lap-band surgery as a "cheat," I think it's more like training wheels. You still have to make the sweeping changes to your diet and exercise habits for the rest of your life, but the band is a built-in accountability tool. Used properly it can help manage appetite and aid portion control—two huge reasons for overeating. Until I learned to do these things for myself, I relied on my "training wheels" to keep me upright.

And despite our inclination to judge how someone else chooses to lose weight, ultimately there is no special prize for doing it alone. The reward is no sweeter if you choose a different path to a healthy weight. Honestly, if there were a surgical option to help people stop smoking or end alcoholism, folks would be signing up in droves, but for some reason people who are over-weight or obese are expected to fly solo. Nonsense, I say.

For me, the cost and risk it involved reinforced my com-mitment to undergo surgery and make the comprehensive life-style changes that would bring me success; I felt I owed it to my family. But perhaps even more important, my commitment to change came from a deep place of surrender. I surrendered the idea that I could, and had to, do this alone. I surrendered the crutch that food had become for me. I surrendered the excuses and the denial. I surrendered the façade that everything was okay. It wasn't.

I wasn't.

Losing weight was the only way out. The pain of change was less than the pain of staying the same.

THE GOWN TIES IN THE BACK: SURGERY AND RECOVERY

Once I decided to have lap-band surgery, the pieces really began to fall into place. Knowing that I'd made this commit-ment, that I had this incredible opportunity, gave me hope. There is a dramatic difference between resolving to try harder (what I had always done in the past) and deciding to change.

The guidelines my surgeon's office gave me included cut-ting back calories immediately (about a month prior to sur-gery). They advise this so that the patient begins to lose weight, thereby shrinking the size of the liver, which sits on top of the stomach. Obese people have supersized internal organs, including the liver. This can be a hindrance during surgery when the doctor needs access to the stomach in order to place the band. Because the procedure is done laparoscopically, there isn't a lot of wiggle room in there. Shrinking the liver allows the surgeon greater precision in placing the band, thereby reducing potential complications.

Two weeks prior to surgery I switched to a mostly liquid diet that included five protein shakes a day and a modest dinner of approximately 300 calories. In the back of my mind it occurred to me that they prescribe this partly to test whether or not you're ready for the dietary guidelines required to succeed with the lap-band. Sometime after my surgery I asked my doctor that question point-blank, and he told me it's not a test per se, and certainly there is a need to minimize the liver's size, but it's a good predictor of long-term success if a patient displays discipline at the outset.

On the morning of surgery I arrived very early. I was nervous but excited. I changed into a surgical gown and took off my fat clothes like I was shedding a skin that represented a former life. The nurses went through the details of the procedure with me and gave my mother, my post-surgery caretaker, all the requisite instruction. I would be groggy and sore, they warned. I would have pain at the five incision sites on my abdomen.

I was thankful to be out during the procedure, and thus blissfully unaware of the two hours it took for my doctor to insert the lap-band through one of the small incisions in my abdomen. He placed the band around the upper one-third of my stomach, and there it will stay, assuming I have no complications, for the rest of my life.

My first impression of the band and how it works was, *This is pure genius!*

If you picture food passing through the opening of a funnel you can see how brilliant this simple device is: depending on the size of the opening (which can be adjusted, hence the device's name: laparoscopic *adjustable* band) and the food itself, the top of the funnel can remain full for quite a while as the contents pass through the opening. This means that dense foods like meats and vegetables will pass through more slowly than thinner or runnier ones such as milk shakes or ice cream. The same is true for all sugar-rich foods like cookies, cake, brownies, and all my other favorites. Here is where a lot of weight-loss surgery patients get themselves into trouble. There are plenty of ways to get around the band. I have even heard patients discussing ways to "outsmart" the band. And this is precisely why

THERE IS A DRAMATIC DIFFERENCE BETWEEN RESOLVING TO TRY HARDER AND DECIDING TO CHANGE.

weight-loss surgery is not a substitute for changed behavior. Those who undermine the effectiveness of this incredible tool do so because they have not made the mental shift to change their behavior for the rest of their lives. They're still looking for a way to cheat the system. As for me, more than eight years postsurgery, I have internalized the lessons learned from the band. Now I eat more slowly, with smaller portion sizes, and eat more frequently throughout the day. I made these lifestyle changes my own, so I have no interest in cheats.

Back on the surgical table, I was groggy upon waking and wondered, *Did they really do it? Is it over?* But of course it was. Nurses helped me move into the recovery area and went over discharge instructions again with my mom. I remember almost none of this.

For the first week following my lap-band surgery, I was prescribed a diet of clear liquids to avoid anything getting stuck in the band while I was still recovering. The following two weeks I was allowed to eat runny foods such as applesauce, yogurt, and soup. Three weeks after the operation, I began to eat normal food again. I was down twenty pounds, which wasn't surprising since I wasn't able to take in a lot of calories while mending from surgery. But it wasn't just that. I had also followed the guidelines given to me by the doctor's office and had heeded the admonition to avoid high-calorie liquids.

In the months that followed, I had my band adjusted several times. Each time a nurse poked me with a needle and injected saline at the site of the port that is attached to my abdominal muscle. The saline travels from the port through a very small tube that is connected to a tiny tube lining the interior of the band. By adding saline, the size of the band's opening is narrowed. While I was busy changing my eating habits— chewing food more thoroughly and eating smaller, healthier meals more frequently throughout the day—the band was constantly reminding me to eat more slowly. The tighter the band, the more slowly food passes through it, and as the band was gradually adjusted over those first few months I had to modify my behavior significantly. I'd always been a fast eater; I think many obese people are. Because the band is a physical barrier, if you eat too much too quickly the food will get stuck. This is something you learn to avoid right away.

Without being overly graphic, food must either go down or come back up. No surprise—down is preferable. As a matter of fact, you really want to avoid "back up" at all costs, for several reasons: it's unpleasant to have food come back up your throat once you've swallowed it (goodness knows we've all experienced that nastiness), but most important, it is dangerous to vomit food up with a lap-band. If it happens with any frequency, the band can loosen and slip out of place. This is a rare but potentially life-threatening situation since this slippage can mean neither solids nor liquids will pass through the band.

Not even your own saliva. Obviously not a good thing. In the first few months after my surgery, I had food come back up, in all its glory, several times. I could no longer eat mindlessly, as it could potentially put my health at risk. I modified my behavior out of necessity, but also because I very much wanted the band to help me be successful.

Once I decided that I was done with weight-loss methods that I knew didn't work for me, like traditional dieting, pills, nutritional counseling, and séances (I'm kidding on that last one, but not much), I was committed to making the band work. Ultimately, it worked because I understood the mechanics of the device, and it made sense to me. It worked because I followed (and continue to follow) all the guidelines established by my doctor. It worked because I put those guidelines into practice—going far beyond my doctor's recommendations and developing hundreds of strategies for healthy eating. It worked because I have become an athlete and exercise vigorously nearly every day. It worked because I did—and continue to do—the very hard work of unraveling how I became obese in the first place. Like so many who are obese, I am an emotional eater, and I have had to confront the powerful negative emotions that I used against myself for decades. Now that I have internalized the lessons I learned from my lap-band, I am able to leave the band in its completely open position, so almost any food passes through unimpeded. I utilized it as a catalyst for change, but I now own the solution.

JOURNEY OF SELF-DISCOVERY

Since having my surgery, I've completely changed my relationship with food. The procedure offered me the tool I needed. I seized the opportunity and ran with it, literally: I became a marathon runner! But more to the point, I envisioned something better for myself. I took action and embraced the change that put my life on an entirely new trajectory.

When I talk about weight loss to people now, I tell them to forget about dieting, forget about deprivation, and even forget about the current buzz of calling it a "lifestyle change." If you're overweight or obese, like I was, nearly everything in your life must be examined because nearly everything you were doing before was making you fat.

Wanting to change, no matter how desperately, is not enough. Dreaming, wishing, hoping, and even praying are not enough. I believe that transformational behavioral change—and make no mistake; that's what we're talking about—is only possible when the pain of staying the same is greater than the pain of change.

Does that mean that everyone must hit rock bottom or have weight-loss surgery before they can lose weight? Absolutely not! But it does mean that you need to embark on a journey of self-discovery, as I did, in order to get your head on straight.

Does it take time? Yes.

Is it hard? Probably harder than you can imagine.

Is it doable? Yes, and hell yes!

Chapter Two

WHERE TO START WHEN YOU DON'T KNOW WHERE TO START

If there is one thing I've learned during my weight-loss journey it's that I'm not terribly exceptional. Oh, don't get me wrong. The fact that I lost over one hundred pounds and have kept it off for more than eight years is remarkable. And I'm not claiming modesty here. I work very hard, and every day I am amazed at what I am capable of. But the truth is, nearly everyone who is overweight or obese has the capacity to accomplish what I have. Most of us are capable of so much more than we give ourselves credit for. I have learned that when I trust myself and live authentically, by no one's rules but my own, I am one seriously tough broad. No illusions though: I am still deeply flawed—I am horribly insecure, have the attention span of a gnat, and procrastinate like a teenager with a term paper due tomorrow morning—but I accept my failings and have learned to make them work for me. You're never going to be without flaws; those heavenly rays of light are not going to shine down on you and change you into some perfect version of yourself. If you're sitting around waiting for that to happen, you're in for a long wait.

I found weight-loss success when I decided that I was unwilling to accept someone else's idea of how I should lose weight. For me, that meant having weight-loss surgery, but it also meant examining nearly every habit, behavior, and belief I held. Our bodies are a reflection of what we do *to* them and *for* them every day. But they're also sort of the endgame of what we believe about ourselves. I had always believed that I should devote myself fully to the care of my husband, my children, and our home. I believed that I should contribute financially to our household income, because how could I be an equal partner if I didn't? And I believed that my feelings of frustration, resentment, anger, and apathy about those roles and about my complete lack of freedom and personal accomplishment were wrong and selfish, since I had taken on all of my responsibilities voluntarily. I would berate myself endlessly by asking, *What the hell do I have to complain about?*

Allowing myself to question some of the assumptions I'd held my whole adult life was terrifying at first. Many of the beliefs we have about ourselves—what we're capable of, what we deserve—are a form of self-definition (e.g., *I am a dutiful wife, I am a working mother*). They help us define ourselves to the world, but they also give us a way to understand ourselves. If I'm a devoted wife and mother, then I'm a good person, and that means that I put my family's needs above my own at all times.

I challenged my long-held beliefs because, even though my rock-bottom experience left me deeply shaken, I realized that accepting other people's definitions of who and what I should be was ultimately dissatisfying and horribly destructive for me.

So when I committed to change I knew I had to not only change my eating and exercise habits, but also change how I saw myself and how I defined myself to the world. Now, even when you recognize that you need to commit to change, it's not like somebody hands you a road map that tells you exactly where to start. But looking back on it now I see my own tentative first steps, and I can see that my transformation was guided by three powerful principles.

Committing to these three guiding principles drove my weight loss. They are simple, yet formidable. Practicing them created a butterfly effect, stirring gale-force changes in my life. Just as the flapping of the butterfly's wings can potentially stir a hurricane on the other side of the world, following these simple principles can bring about colossal change.

So, where do you start when you don't know where to start? You commit to these three principles. I may not have had a road map when I started, but now that I've bushwhacked my way through the weight-loss jungle, I've got one, and I want to share it with you.

GUIDING PRINCIPLE #1: BE WILLING TO DIG DEEP

For years I stood up at all of those political rallies and speeches, feeling like a complete and utter embarrassment and fraud. Accepting other people's definitions of what made a good person left me feeling empty and unworthy. I felt deceitful, like a phony. These feelings flooded me with a host of negative emotions. Guess what I did with those negative emotions. Yep, stuffed 'em down. Literally. It wasn't even episodic, as in something specific would trigger it and I'd binge eat in reaction; I had a level of frustration and anxiety that was constant and drove me to food as an outlet to cope. It's a pattern I see so clearly in myself now, yet it wasn't until I stripped away the façade of trying to be perfect at everything, for everybody, that I was able to cut through the denial that kept me trapped in that behavior.

ATTENDING A SOCIAL FUNCTION IS JUST THE OPPORTUNITY, NOT THE REASON, WE CHOOSE TO OVEREAT.

Digging deep means looking for those patterns in yourself. You'll probably find, as I did, that you must look beyond the obvious triggers. Sure, going out with the gang after work for happy hour or attending a family barbecue is a challenge, but that's just the opportunity to eat, not the reason you're choosing to overeat. Be willing to look for the deeper reason and then be willing to challenge that reason. Do you feel trapped in your job? Are you living on the edge financially? Do you suffer from chronic health challenges? Whatever it is, you are entitled to those feelings and exploring them is worthwhile. Doing something about them is even better.

Bottom line: You are capable of so much more than you may believe at this moment. If you need help exploring those long-standing issues that set off emotional eating, consider a professional therapist who can help you identify negative behavior patterns and offer practical strategies to turn them around.

GUIDING PRINCIPLE #2: CREATE A VISION FOR YOURSELF

At my heaviest I often felt as though I lived in a paradoxical state in which I was the most conspicuous and yet the most invisible person in the room at any time. I would walk into clothing stores to look around and feel everyone's eyes on me, sizing me up. *Wow, she's huge!* I imagined them thinking. *What could she possibly find in here to fit her?* I felt scrutiny and judgment directed at me all of the time because I was usually the fattest person in the room no matter where I went.

Even sitting on the couch at home watching sporting events could be painful. We'd be watching our beloved Seattle Seahawks on a Sunday afternoon, and they would have all the players' stats on the screen—yards gained, pass completions, height, and, of course, weight. I outweighed all of them. These are NFL players we're talking about. Yeah, that was depressing.

Strangely, when I didn't feel like I was being stared at or judged, I felt invisible. Not only does being fat make you uncomfortable, it makes *those around you* uncomfortable. It felt as though people looked right through me, or averted their eyes because they were embarrassed for me. This strange duality of being the most conspicuous and the least-acknowledged person everywhere I went was so destructive, and it ate away at my self-esteem.

When I had my epiphany I realized I had suffered long enough and felt sure that I deserved better than that. My vision for myself was very simple, really; I just wanted to be normal. I didn't need to be thin or beautiful. I didn't need to be the center of attention. I wanted to feel acknowledged, but not be a source of curiosity. I wanted to shop in stores with "normal" sizes, without being the subject of scrutiny or derision. I wanted to move through the world as a regular-sized person. To be sure, it was a rather modest vision, but at the time it seemed distant and damned near impossible.

That vision, simple as it was, became a driving force for me. As you move forward in your own weight-loss journey I encourage you to explore the vision you have for your own future. A vision board—a collage of images and words meant to visually portray the future you want for yourself—is a popular tool for people pursuing a big goal like weight loss. Collecting and sharing inspiring photos, quotes, and images is the basis for Pinterest, a pinboard-style content-sharing service that allows the user to create theme-based collections of "pins." It is a great way to create a twenty-first-century vision board. Because I'm a very visual person I find it extremely helpful to let pictures guide my ambitions. I collect images and quotes that represent for me the feeling I want to achieve: satisfaction, accomplishment, contentment, happiness, joy. My own weight-loss vision board was less about pictures of supermodels in bikinis, and more about women who looked happy in their own skin. These weren't women who epitomized some idealized body image; instead they were women who just looked happy, engaged, fulfilled. I so longed to be one of them. Eventually, my goals would move in the direction of refining muscle tone or wearing a hot red dress, but in the beginning my ambition was simply to feel normal.

Bottom line: Be honest with yourself about what you want and why. Having a vision for where you're going means you're moving toward something positive. As Steve Jobs famously said, "If you are working on

something exciting that you really care about, you don't
have to be pushed. The vision pulls you."
He's so right; believe him.

GUIDING PRINCIPLE #3: EMBRACE CHANGE

Accept that this is not going to be easy. You're not looking for
a quick fix. This is not a situation where you can grit your teeth
and tough it out for a couple of weeks. You already tried the
thirty-day boot camp, the three-day cleanse, and the four-hour
diet. You've already tried all that stuff that doesn't work. I did
too.

It's time to embrace change for the rest of your life. If
change were easy, no one would ever get stuck. Look around
you—most people are stuck on something. Overcoming the
status quo will take courage and determination. Acknowledge
that now or you will fail again.

A decade or so before I finally lost weight, in the midst
of one of my more earnest attempts at dieting, I enlisted the
help of a nutritional counselor. She was a sort of hybrid nutri-
tionist and behavioral coach who had me record what I ate for
the week and then take it to her for examination and review.
She and I would go over the journal in detail, talking through
my successes and setbacks. This might have been a very helpful approach if I'd been ready to meet her halfway. Certainly, I
wanted to lose weight. I wished, hoped, and even prayed I'd lose
weight. But as we all know, if that were enough, who'd be fat?

I remember the counselor saying to me at the very beginning of our first session, "This is going to be a lot of work. Are
you prepared for this kind of change to your lifestyle?" I was
about fifty pounds overweight at the time and hoping to get
pregnant again, but reluctant to do so because I knew from

experience how hard pregnancy was on my body. I knew it would mean even more weight gain.

"Well, honestly," I confessed to her, "I'm not sure. I pretty much like my life the way it is. I just don't want to be fat." Ah, if only! If only I could have continued to eat whatever I wanted (my modus operandi at the time), whenever I wanted, as much as I wanted . . . and just not continue to gain weight. She let out a big sigh and, though she retained her professional demeanor, gave me a look that said, "C'mon, lady! Work with me here!"

No surprise that I didn't last long with her. She meant serious business, and I was far from being ready to change. I endured another decade of being fat, and added another seventy pounds to my body, before I found the courage to change.

Some of us are slow learners.

Embracing change means that you stop clinging to the habits, behaviors, and attitudes that got you into this mess. While that paradigm shift won't necessarily make you immune to the pull of the cake at the monthly office birthday celebration, you will look at it differently. You will no longer see it as a delicious treat that is a welcome break, well deserved because you work so hard and give so much to so many; instead you will see it as a distraction from your goals and your values. There is no reason for you to run and hide from it, so you can still socialize with everyone and certainly wish a happy birthday to those special people you're celebrating, but the cake itself will hold no power over you.

Does that seem impossible from where you sit? I get that. I too would've sneered and laughed at that idea 120 pounds ago. It won't seem impossible to you by the time you finish this book, though; I promise.

Bottom line: Forget the "ten easy tips and tricks" approach that you see on magazine covers; successful permanent weight loss means changing your habits forever.

Where you start, when you don't know where to start, is by committing to being honest and compassionate with yourself. Just like me, you are absolutely capable of transforming your body, your health, and your life. If you're willing to dig deep, create a personally meaningful vision, and embrace change, you may actually experience something akin to those heavenly clouds parting and the choirs of angels singing. Because when you recognize, as I did, that you deserve all the joy and happiness you can garner in this life, there are a whole lot of good things that come your way. And ultimately, that's what it's all about. Weight loss is just the by-product.

Good grief, life is short. What are we waiting for?! Let's go get it!

Chapter Three

THE ROOT OF EMOTIONAL EATING: DENIAL, FEAR, HOPELESSNESS, AND SHAME

A willingness to dig deep, create a personally meaningful vision, and embrace change is predicated on one thing: self-awareness. My self-awareness was a gift I didn't ask for, and truthfully didn't even know I lacked. It was thrust upon me when I realized that trying to be all things to all people—except myself—made me miserable. Recognizing that I deserved better than living in misery was my awakening. And upon awakening I was forced to confront the emotional eating that kept me locked in self-destruction.

People who've never struggled with their weight are often puzzled by why anyone would ever eat themselves into obesity. Why not just stop eating when you're no longer hungry? Whatever excuses or reasoning a person might trot out to explain their difficulty with losing weight—slow metabolism, no time to work out, genetic predisposition—you don't get to be obese without eating way too much food. But why? Why would someone keep eating and eating, beyond physical hunger? When it's making them sick and miserable? When it's costing them so much?

As I said in chapter one, obesity isn't an intellectual problem; fat people aren't fat because they're stupid. For me, and I suspect for a great many people who struggle with obesity, the root of my inability to stop eating and my never-ending battle with my body was deeply, profoundly emotional.

This is why it makes me furious when I hear so-called diet and fitness experts doling out overly simplistic advice that addresses the behaviors that lead to obesity without addressing the root cause of those behaviors. This is the catch-22 of dieting: almost any popular diet will work if you stick to it. It's in that enormous "if" that the real problem lies. Looking at weight loss on a purely symptomatic level is like thinking someone might be cured of a sinus infection by giving them a tissue.

LOOKING AT WEIGHT LOSS ON A PURELY SYMPTOMATIC LEVEL IS LIKE THINKING SOMEONE MIGHT BE CURED OF A SINUS INFECTION BY GIVING THEM A TISSUE.

Have you ever met an overweight person who has *never* been on a diet? Of course not! More likely, they've tried every diet on the planet, just like I did. Yet diets—no matter how clever, how regimented, how perfectly conceived—can never make a dent in the denial, fear, hopelessness, and shame that push so many of us to eat well beyond the point of satiety (hell, of *sanity!*) in the first place. For me, until my emotional prison finally started to crumble, my weight was going nowhere but up.

DROWNING IN DENIAL

As a young mother, I was preoccupied with my children's development, well-being, and happiness. I shifted gears, as many of us do when we become parents, from the self-care that occupies us in our teens and twenties to the caretaking of others that consumes our time as we build a family. Perhaps it is because I am a nurturer at heart, a people pleaser, and, I suppose, a traditionalist, that I willingly embraced a June Cleaver existence rather than carving out a life based on a personal vision that I had for myself.

In the absence of a personal agenda, meeting my family's needs became my overriding objective. As I've said, I wrapped myself completely in the roles of mother, wife, community and church volunteer, and, of course, political spouse. For my efforts I was rewarded with the positive reinforcement I desperately craved. And yet I felt utterly empty.

Though the particular circumstances differ from person to person, I hear this same scenario repeated again and again by others who are plagued by emotional eating.

We feel empty. We feel trapped. We are consumed by inner turmoil. There is nowhere to hide from these feelings. We struggle to cope. Emotional eating is a coping mechanism to deal with powerful feelings that are too difficult to face. We stuff the feelings down in an effort to push them away—or worse yet, our discontent does not even rise to the level of consciousness. The thoughts are so troublesome, and probably so deeply buried, that we are not even consciously aware of their existence.

At its core, emotional eating *is* denial.

Somewhere in the course of my beleaguered food life, I learned to detach from unpleasant feelings by mindlessly eating. This behavior became a way to quiet troublesome thoughts and, eventually, to stem the physical and mental distress of obesity itself. The sensations of my physical body (discomfort, pain) coupled with the interminable anxiety that was triggered by my unhappiness about my life circumstances and my weight were too difficult for me to confront. The only way I knew how to cope was to push those feelings away, or, more accurately, to stuff them down.

It wasn't so much that I was in denial about the weight itself. The physical reality of obesity was impossible to ignore. I would step on the scale three days a week, just as I do now, and I would observe the numbers creeping up and up. I felt my clothes get tighter and tighter. In fact, the only thing getting smaller was my hope that I might ever turn this around.

Over time, I slowly became the elephant in the room. The one you cannot look at, yet cannot ignore.

Denial looks different for everyone. I know from interactions with friends and readers that it comes in many guises. I heard from someone recently who told me she only steps on a scale once a year at the doctor's office because she cannot face that number. "It messes with my head!" she said defensively. I tried to point out the flaw in this line of thinking as gently as I could, to no avail. Denial 1, reality 0.

Others deny their inability to control their consumption of certain foods. They bring unhealthy "treat" foods into their home under the pretense that they are for their children or spouse. They may actually believe that they will be able to resist. And after all, why should their family be deprived of treats just because they cannot control their food impulses? So they violate one of my prime weight-loss directives—which you will hear more about in chapter six—and allow unhealthy food to cross their threshold. Then (surprise, surprise), they eat it.

I lived this particular type of denial every Sunday when I went to the grocery store. Knowing full well I could not control my compulsion to eat unhealthy foods, I'd buy them anyway, pretending that the goldfish crackers and ice cream sandwiches were for the kids, and the bagels and cream cheese were for my husband. I knew I had no willpower around these foods, and yet I would bring them into my home. Week after week. Month after month. Year after year.

In fact, I was swimming in a river of denial for years. For me, denial meant detachment. Detachment from my physical body, detachment from what I was doing to myself, detachment from the misery I suffered yet felt hopeless to overcome.

Detachment from my physical body meant disengaging from what I looked like. Of course, I knew what I looked like—there were occasional photos that I could not avoid, though I tried very hard—but I almost never looked in a mirror except to apply makeup and check my hair. That is to say, I almost never looked at myself below the neck. I simply couldn't. If I didn't look at my body, then my obesity didn't exist, right? My disgust and humiliation with my physical appearance ran so deep that I could not face it; in fact, I put up a wall in my mind so that I could not "see" it. That wall was my defense, albeit a shaky one, against the self-loathing I feared would paralyze me if I forced myself to really look at my physical body.

I dressed in the dark, or alone. I turned away from mirrors and my reflection in windows. I averted my eyes in instances where it was impossible to avoid seeing myself. This self-denial becomes reflexive and is incalculably destructive. When you deny your physical body, you feel invisible—or at least you wish you were invisible. When I look at some of the few photographs that exist of me at my heaviest I can see it in my own eyes: I am apologetic for others' having to look at me, apologetic for taking up space.

What a horrible way to live.

My denial also manifested as detachment from what I was doing to myself. I don't pretend to be qualified to diagnose anyone, even myself, as having an eating disorder, but I will admit to disordered eating. I ate in a way that can only be described as such. In fact, when people ask me how I lost the weight, the most straightforward answer I can give is that I stopped using food inappropriately.

WHEN PEOPLE ASK ME HOW I LOST THE WEIGHT, THE MOST STRAIGHTFORWARD ANSWER I CAN GIVE IS THAT I STOPPED USING FOOD INAPPROPRIATELY.

Using food inappropriately meant that I would stand in my pantry, or in front of my refrigerator, and eat . . . and eat . . . and eat . . . until I could eat no more. Alone, always alone, I would consume food as though it might slip through my grasp: cookies, cheese, crackers, chips, ice cream—anything. *Everything.*

In saner moments, I would kick myself for my lack of discipline when I was engaged in this manic behavior. I'd berate myself for being "weak" and "pathetic" because I could not control myself. I'd promise myself that I'd never, ever do it again. That I'd be "good" from here on out.

And yet, I wasn't.

I'd do it again: stand in the pantry and shovel in food until that voice would call out to me, saying, *Stop doing this! You don't want to do this!* And then I'd remember the promise I made to myself. And I'd feel like shit all over again.

I'd mindlessly eat thousands of calories this way. After a few minutes of this, I certainly wasn't hungry any longer, at least not for food. I was desperate to push down my feelings, feelings I was much too scared to start unraveling. During these binges, it was almost as though I would leave my body while I was eating. I would detach from myself and attempt to soothe my churning anxiety with the salty, sweet, fatty flavor combinations I craved.

While I disengaged from my physical body and pretended not to notice the damage I did to myself over and over again with food, the most destructive manifestation of my denial was the detachment I felt from my conflicted misery in my role as wife and mom.

It's extremely difficult for me to admit, even now, how unhappy I was about being a full-time caregiver. As anyone who's had that role knows, the word *caregiver* fails to capture the depth and breadth of your immersion. It is a complete consumption of your mental and physical energy. In my case, it overwhelmed me. It swallowed me. I surrendered to it voluntarily—I chose to become a wife, mother, nurturer, volunteer, and homemaker—yet it slowly suffocated me. I was unable to resolve this fundamental conflict in my life: I had chosen my circumstances willingly, yet their very nature left me desperately unhappy. I was isolated, I was desolate, and, in fact, I was deeply depressed.

Certainly not everyone who makes the same life choices I did ends up depressed and obese. And plenty of people find themselves depressed and/or obese who made life choices that were entirely different from mine. But among emotional eaters runs this common thread: we feel hopelessness about changing our circumstances and are unwilling to admit the deep-seated conflicts we face.

By nature, we find ways as human beings to protect ourselves from threats. And calling into question the validity of major life choices, especially those we feel hopeless to change, is a threat. After all, if you can't change it, why look at it? Better to keep your head in the sand and deny it. On some level, then, denial makes complete sense, at least as a means of self-preservation.

Although I had a life that looked perfect from the outside—perfect husband, perfect children, perfect house, perfect job—on the inside I was desperately unhappy yet unable to face it. That inability to face my circumstances, that denial, could have killed me.

I don't do anything half-assed. Including drowning in denial.

FEAR FACTOR

At the heart of my struggles was a deep, unrelenting fear. Obviously, I'm not talking about fear of physical danger. I'm talking about apprehension, worry, dread, anxiety, even panic. Emotional fear.

Psychologists make distinctions among these terms, but for the purposes of discussing emotional eating I'm going to lump them together. If my doing so isn't in total alignment with the American Psychological Association's definitions, I apologize. My expertise with these emotions is on the receiving end, not the diagnostic end.

When I was growing up in the 1960s and 1970s, the extent of my vision for myself was being married and having kids. I didn't aspire to anything beyond the traditional role that society decided was a good blueprint for a woman's life. Back then, of course, there were plenty of women who had their own dreams and aspirations beyond family life, but I wasn't one of them. During my rather geographically and emotionally untethered childhood, my mom and I moved around constantly. After a parade of Mom's boyfriends, husbands, and relationship dramas, I desperately wanted the stability and security of a traditional life. Conveniently, assuming a traditional role—marriage, children, deference to my husband's goals—also granted me the validation I craved. I wanted to do the things I thought I "should" do, things everyone would approve of.

Following this course meant that I could avoid what I refer to as the "triple Ds": disapproval, derision, and disappointing others. These three competed for top billing on my list of fears. I spent a lifetime—and most of my mental and emotional energy—doing everything in my power to dodge them. The underlying fear that drove the triple Ds was that I wasn't good enough just the way I was. As a child, love always felt conditional to me; if I got good grades, if I behaved, then I was acceptable. In my family, love was granted based on what you did, not because of who you were. My fear of rejection and abandonment if I fell short of others' expectations kept me desperately chasing that elusive validation.

And despite my having chosen the glorified path of marriage and motherhood, once I was deep into the life I'd envisioned for myself it wasn't fitting me very well. In fact, despite how deeply I loved my family, my lack of any kind of personal aspirations or individual achievements gnawed away at me day by day. But confronting this? Admitting that this life wasn't making me happy? That was inconceivable—terrifying even.

I found respite from this unrelenting fear, this oppressive anxiety, only in the oblivion that happened when I binge ate. It's no surprise that when you're trapped in this kind of emotional snare and cope with it by self-medicating with food, dieting seems impossible. I was barely hanging on even *with* turning to food for comfort. Denying myself that coping mechanism was unthinkable. I used to tell people that dieting felt like being underwater; I could do it for a little while, but sooner or later I had to come up for air. Food was my air.

While food helped me hide from the triple Ds I feared, my weight became its own place to hide. The bigger I got, the more I internalized my fear and underlying unhappiness, and as a result I became more isolated. My size became its own reason not to participate in life. In fact, as I got bigger, my comfort zone got smaller and smaller. My weight became a scapegoat for everything that I did not want to—or could not—face.

AS I GOT BIGGER, MY COMFORT ZONE GOT SMALLER AND SMALLER.

More than just a scapegoat though, it was also my security blanket. Passive acceptance of my weight and my life circumstances meant I didn't need to challenge my dysfunctional eating behavior. If I faced my fears, called my decisions into question, I would be forced to stop relying on the binge eating that relieved my stress. As much as I hoped and dreamed that someday I could be that person who did not turn to pizza and cheesecake as a pressure relief valve, did that mean I could never eat pizza and cheesecake ever again? That seemed inconceivable! As much as I loathed my own behavior—burying my head in the sand of denial, pushing away anxiety by stuffing it down with food—the escape that emotional eating offered seemed the only available solution. After all, even though food doesn't offer validation, it is a solace of sorts. A comfort. Food doesn't judge. It doesn't care if you never amount to anything. And it won't leave you if you screw up.

And yet, nobody had to tell me that the toll this behavior was taking on me was brutal, both from a physical and psychological standpoint. The vicious cycle held me in its grip; I was held captive by fear and anxiety . . . which I coped with by overeating . . . which led to more fear and anxiety.

Since having my lap-band surgery and losing weight, I have devised strategies that help me deal with fear. But no matter what method of weight loss you choose, you can't just decide not to feel fear anymore. I'm still a worrier. I'm still dogged by self-doubt at times. I still fear the triple Ds (disapproval, derision, and disappointing others).

What I don't do anymore is stuff those feelings down with food. If, like me, you're conditioned to turn to food when you're afraid (or anxious or stressed), you may always be inclined to feel that way. But that doesn't mean we're condemned to the behavior. Emotional eating is a learned behavior. I have unlearned it, and so can you.

HOPELESSNESS: THE QUIET ENEMY

It's not as if nobody's ever written about emotional eating before. Even many mainstream diets occasionally touch on it in their programs. Some might talk about stress eating or eating out of boredom. They may even address some of the shame involved in obesity. But what they rarely talk about—and what is absolutely vital to understand in turning around emotional eating—is hopelessness. From my experience, understanding this pervasive, pernicious emotion is critical to turning around emotional eating habits. My hopelessness, which gave way to futility, was why my obesity became an entrenched lifestyle.

Walk with me through the mall food court and I will illustrate.

That smell . . . Lordy. You know it, don't you? Yeah, me too.

Here's the conversation that I'd have with myself when I was fat and was assaulted by that smell:

Oh my God, CINNABON! It smells sooooooooooo good. And I could really use a pick-me-up. Yes! Yes! YES!!

Knock it off! You don't need that cinnamon roll and it's not on your diet! You promised yourself you weren't gonna eat crap like that anymore!

Oh shut up, you annoying buzzkill! Why must you suck the fun out of everything?!

This entire conversation would go on inside my head in the space of a nanosecond as I approached the Cinnabon store in my mall's food court. The food court (or, more accurately, the *food carnival*) is an extravaganza of enticing sights, sounds, and smells. The granddaddy of them all is Cinnabon. Occasionally, I would white-knuckle it past the place and avoid the siren's call. Very often I would not. The reason I would give in to Cinnabon was not just because the smell was so enticing. (It was.) It wasn't just because it tasted so damn good. (It did.) I'd give in and get the Cinnabon because I had no reason not to.

Oh, I was dieting . . . again . . . always. But that wasn't a compelling enough reason. I knew it was bad for me. I was fat, not stupid. I have a master's degree. Like I said, obesity isn't an intellectual problem. It's just that those reasons weren't enough. I had no hope of resisting because deep-seated resignation about my weight and my life circumstances had taken hold. Resistance was futile. In short, I felt hopeless, and here's why.

For years, decades really, I had virtually no interests, friends, or activities that didn't involve my children. I didn't have the confidence to claim anything for myself, so I inhabited a role that granted me status and virtue by default. Problem is, that role left me feeling desperately empty much of the time.

Meanwhile, we spent our lives like many families do, on the precipice of a financial cliff. We were middle class, but with four active kids in relatively high-cost-of-living suburban Seattle, money was always tight. Like most moms, I've moved in and out of the workforce over the years; I have been a full-time stay-at-home mom, a full-time working mom, a part-time working mom, and a small business owner. Each of these scenarios brought its own stressors, but maybe the most challenging of all were the years I spent running a state-licensed day care in our home.

My very long days were spent tending to the needs of a half dozen children in addition to my own and operating a small business. To say that these years were difficult and dissatisfying would be a gross understatement. I had my reasons for not wanting to put my own children in a day care, but the burden of being tied to the care of so many—and the fact that I disliked it so much—meant that I ran at a happiness deficit for a very

long time. It was more than just a lack of happiness: I was operating without pleasure of any kind.

Other than food.

I know I am not alone in this happiness deficit. We all
live hectic, stressful lives. Many of us worry constantly about
financial pressures, and because of that we feel trapped by our
circumstances. Our jobs and our children, the very choices we
have made, make it seem impossible to change anything. We
have obligations: a mortgage to pay, a family to support, car
payments to keep up with, health concerns that mean we need
insurance coverage we can only get from an employer. The list
is endless.

So when I approached Cinnabon in the mall food court
and that argument played out in my head, the voice that urged
me to indulge usually won. That voice won because she was
loud and insistent:

You never get to have anything of your own.

Nobody ever does anything for you.

Have this one little treat. It will make you feel better.

And it did, of course. For a fleeting moment.

And then it didn't.

That's the way emotional eating works though, right?
You go up the roller coaster, and it all feels good and exciting
and you think you can control it, and then you drop ten stories at the speed of light and are whipped around until you're
nauseated.

The same internal voice that told me to indulge in Cinnabon
had me convinced that my situation was hopeless, so I might
as well grab a little happiness where I could. What she didn't
tell me was that surrendering to this hopelessness over and
over again would lead to deeply entrenched futility. Futility is
a powerful force that kept me stuck in a destructive pattern for

a very long time. I was left with a resignation that my situation would never get better. That *I* would never get better.

When everything came crashing down around me in 2007, it was my turning point. Hope is a funny thing; it doesn't always come from a bright, sunny place. Sometimes it comes from a pile of rubble. Amid the wreckage—failing at my job as a para-legal, letting my husband and family down, my weight spiraling out of control—I saw myself standing on a cliff. The path I had been on for so many years had fallen out from under me. I was

BEING WILLING TO CONFRONT AND THEN ACTIVELY CHANGE SOME OF THE LIFE CIRCUMSTANCES THAT MADE ME FEEL TRAPPED AND UNHAPPY WAS PIVOTAL TO MY WEIGHT-LOSS SUCCESS.

on a precipice with no stable footing. Simply put, I could not take another step in the life I was living.

That realization was a clarion call for me. Hearing a clarion call is a pivotal moment in your life when an answer you need becomes brilliantly clear. When the clarion sounds, you have the choice to take action or not.

I chose action.

I chose a new path.

I talked to my family and my doctor. I had lap-band sur-gery, but even before the surgery I started eating much bet-ter. I was still at the start of my journey, but the clarion call reverberated far beyond taking control of my weight. I started saying no to other people's demands and expectations, and learned to set boundaries. I created hundreds of strategies to help me make consistently healthy food choices, and I found a joy in moving my body that can never be found in a box of Oreos. In short, I seized control of my life, and I have never let go. In seizing control—of the big decisions about how I spend my time and the smaller ones about food choices and how I exercise—I found hope.

I don't feel the pull to indulge at food courts anymore because I now have a reason not to. That reason is hope. Hope that my future cannot possibly be as dark as my past. Hope that my future is mine to determine.

Just as hopelessness gives way to futility, hope engenders optimism. As Pollyanna as it may sound, every day I am now filled with a sunny optimism for the possibilities that lie before me. Being willing to confront *and then actively change* some of the life circumstances that made me feel trapped and unhappy was pivotal to my weight-loss success. In fact, I'd go so far as to say that the weight-loss surgery wouldn't have mattered for squat if I hadn't been willing to face my unhappiness and make peace with my true feelings.

If you turn to food to cope with stress, resentment, anger, frustration, or any of a thousand other emotions like I did, how can you possibly expect to stick to a diet without changing those underlying problems?

You can't.

You won't.

Hopelessness and futility could have done me in. They are the reason millions of people fail at weight loss, time and time again.

SHAME ON YOU

In my estimation, shame runs along a spectrum. At one end is shyness, then discouragement, embarrassment, self-consciousness, and finally humiliation. We think of shame as something you do *to* somebody:

"Shame on you!"

"You should be ashamed of yourself!"

But truthfully, shame is a self-inflicted wound. It's a dirty lens through which you see yourself. No matter what you achieve or accomplish, the achievement is instantly diminished because your vision is distorted. Your own thoughts play cruel tricks on you. There is no respite from your negative internal dialogue, because even if someone offers reassurance or congratulations, you don't really believe them.

This stuff hits me where I live. On a scale of zero shame to 10—which is basically curled up in the fetal position—I spent much of my adult life at about a 6.5, but I had days when I was totally in the red zone.

For as long as I can remember, I was afraid I wasn't good enough just as myself. Somewhere in my subconscious, I decided that if other people approved of me then it meant I had value as a person. Where exactly this comes from I have no idea. In my case, I was never physically abused or traumatized; I always knew my parents loved me. Oh, we had our issues to be sure. As I've said, my parents divorced when I was in elementary school. Because Mom and I moved around a lot, I went to a different school every year between fifth and tenth grade. As a preteen and teenager I had a series of stepparents, most of whom were caring people, though the emotionally abusive stepfather I mentioned earlier was the cruel exception. Still, we were middle class, and I knew very little physical hardship. There was always food on the table and a roof over my head.

Somehow, knowing all of that made me feel worse as I battled my demons. What did I have to feel bad about? What right did I have to feel so unhappy? Guilt on top of shame. Great.

There was, however, a lot of manic behavior surrounding food in my childhood. When I look back at it now it seems dysfunctional, but when you're a kid you just go with it because it's all you know. My mother was a lifelong yo-yo dieter who herself had been raised in a home with lots of shame around food and body image. I think our parents often try to spare us the pain they think we'll experience if we're overweight by cajoling us to conform. They may use guilt, fear, blame, ridicule, and criticism as their tools. My mother used those tools on me, as her mother had used them on her. Mine used to say, "Someday you'll care enough about yourself not to eat like that" after I'd eaten something I "shouldn't" have eaten. She carted me off to my first Weight Watchers meeting when I was ten years old. There was always this oppressive feeling that, because of my weight, there was something wrong with me. In retrospect, I'm sure Mom's heart was in the right place and that she wanted to protect me from the lifelong cage match she'd been in with her body; like most parents, she just wanted better for me. Fear of food was a legacy that was passed down through generations in my family. Maybe in yours as well.

My mother's manic, dysfunctional eating and the shame surrounding that behavior were part of a deep-rooted legacy that was wrapped around me like a newborn's swaddling blanket. In our household, food was the enemy. For much of my childhood it was just my mom and me. My mother's life as a single parent couldn't have been easy. She used food as a coping mechanism to deal with stress and unhappiness, just as I would go on to do, particularly when she was in an "off" cycle of her never-ending on-off dieting. She had the same weaknesses for sweet, sugary foods that I do and would often bake treats but then hide them from me so I wouldn't overeat them. She passed it off as kind of a funny family quirk—"Remember that time I hid the pie in the washing machine?"—but the message was clear: Eating was something to be hidden. Eating was shameful.

From my adult vantage point, and with the insight I gained through seeing a therapist, I see that the shame surrounding my eating habits and my body image came from all of these sources: my mother's manic eating behavior, the cruel emotional abuse I suffered at the hands of my stepfather, the clear message that love was conditional, and the distorted thinking that is borne out of all of these cumulative injuries.

My deep shame around eating and body issues may have started in childhood, but it certainly didn't end there. As the obese wife of a very public man, I was ashamed not only of my body but of what I thought it communicated to the world about me: that I was unable to control myself, that I was undisciplined, that I was weak and hopelessly flawed. I felt judged by everyone who looked at me or, more accurately, looked through me. I avoided going to public events with Rob whenever possible for fear of being uncomfortable and even of reflecting poorly on him. Having four kids at home provided all the excuse I needed to get out of doing just about anything; I could opt out in the name of being a good mom, and no one would question me.

Besides avoiding events where I'd be especially visible or (gasp!) have my picture taken, I naturally avoided activities where I knew I'd have to do something physical—field day at the kids' school, horseback riding with a Scout troop, rock climbing with a church group. When one of the older kids had an activity along those lines, I'd send Rob or enlist another parent to cover for me, hiding behind my youngest children, saying they were too little to participate and needed me to stay home with them.

Of course, I couldn't anticipate every threat to my self-esteem, and occasionally, I would be publicly humiliated despite my vigilant attempts to avoid it.

One year when my youngest children were very little, I remember taking them to get their picture taken with Santa at the mall. We stood in line for hours, along with everyone else, which did not improve the mood of my youngest, a toddler. When we finally reached the front of the line, the elves and I arranged the kids on and around Santa, with said cranky toddler front and center. I did my best to forestall the seemingly inevitable tantrum, assuring him that he was okay and encouraging them all to smile. I went to whisper something reassuring into my littlest one's ear, but then found that I could not get back up. I was so physically unwieldy that I could not manage my own body weight. Naturally, everyone in line could see, and a few compassionate souls nearby helped me up, kind

SHAME IS A WOUND THAT NEVER HEALS BECAUSE IT IS RIPPED OPEN OVER AND OVER AGAIN.

in their concern. But my humiliation was beyond words. I was mortified that I should need this kind of help to do something as simple as getting to my feet, as though I were an elderly person rather than a young mother. I was awash in shame.

These are the degradations obese people face daily. Shame is a wound that never heals because it is ripped open over and over again. It is a pain I cannot describe and would not wish on another living soul. If you have experiences like this and have turned to food to cope, you know all too well what I mean. Intuitively, I'm sure you also know that no diet alone can fix this.

But it is fixable.

Chapter Four

DIGGING OUT OF EMOTIONAL EATING
AND RECLAIMING OURSELVES

Emotional eating was my way of pushing away uncomfortable issues—the loneliness and isolation I felt at
home, the stress about measuring up to others' expectations, and the pressure to be the "perfect" political wife—but
it also had become a habit in my life. Certainly my lap-band
offered help in terms of managing my hunger and downsizing
my portions, but emotional eating is so much more than that.
In order to make a dent in this lifelong eating behavior, I knew
I had to set aside the excuses and self-destructive habits I'd
clung to for years. As I moved forward I vowed to keep these
three promises to myself:

1. **Be honest with myself.**
   I knew that this journey would require me to be utterly truthful about who I am and what I believe. I vowed to face my reality head-on.

2. **Try my best.**
   So many times before I'd failed because I cut myself too much slack. *I'm tired. I've had a bad day. I'm on vacation!* But to effect long-lasting change, I knew I needed to strive to be the best version of myself every single day. In my heart of hearts I knew I deserved nothing less.

BE HONEST WITH YOURSELF, TRY YOUR BEST, AND SEEK OUT HELP.

---

3. **Seek out help.**
   I had to come to terms with the fact that I needed help. Trying to lose weight for decades on my own got me nowhere but heavier and more depressed. I finally realized that there's no special prize at the end if you do it alone.

LIVING LIKE IT MATTERS

Though the current popular catchphrase "lifestyle change" alludes to the scope of the shift that's necessary for weight loss, most of us still isolate weight from everything else in our lives. That is, we think that what we eat and how we move are independent of all the other things in our lives: our relationships, our job, and our leisure activities. What I learned, though, is that they're not.

Part of reclaiming myself was looking at how I spent my time and learning to be more proactive in establishing boundaries. As you'll read in this chapter, I was a people pleaser for lots of reasons, but in my life before weight loss, there wasn't much pleasure in it for me. I worked my way from feeling invisible, to asserting my wishes to my family and friends, to now taking on the world and living without regret. In the first phase of this change I called my campaign Doormat No More! (Just in my own head. You can't go around proclaiming it at PTA meetings or people will look at you funny.) It was a good reminder that I didn't need to be everybody's everything. And it afforded me the courage I needed to reclaim my life.

The rest of this book is a glimpse into a thousand paradigm shifts that I experienced along the way as I transformed my body and my life. I had to question every assumption I made about my life: how I spent my time and my money, what I did for a living, and who I spent my time with. It forced me to scrutinize my beliefs and values and then structure new habits that were aligned with those beliefs and values. I looked hard at myself—all of myself, good and bad—and made an honest assessment of who I really am and what I'm made of. From where I sit now it seems clear that the real reason I have been successful at long-term weight loss is not because I had lap-band surgery. It is because I take that hard look at myself every single day. And I refuse to look away.

The epiphany I had in 2007, when I chose surgery and committed to changing my eating and exercise behaviors for life, was a realization that, of all the things that seemed out of control in my life, my weight was at the vortex.

And even though I feared what all addicts fear—letting go of the one thing they've found that seems to soothe the deep existential dread (be it alcohol, gambling, or, in my case, food)—I knew at my core that this behavior was going to kill me. I had to let it go.

As I learned to let go of food as a coping mechanism and put it back in its proper place as nourishment, I had to learn to sit with my feelings. I had to learn new coping mechanisms and new strategies to deal with the barrage of negative feelings that drove me to overeat for most of my life. It's important to acknowledge that I didn't do it alone; I sought out a professional therapist to help me work through my childhood issues and my fears. All of those complex emotions were right under the surface, and when I no longer stuffed them down with food, they came pouring out. My husband and I also saw a marriage counselor to help us better understand how we could improve our communication. Our new commitment to openness and honesty—even when the issues are painful—has brought us renewed intimacy.

Now, eating like it matters is part of how I *live* like it matters. Every day, when my feet hit the floor, I commit to the same things I ask you to commit to: be honest with yourself, try your best, and seek out help. It's a difficult journey, but it's also tremendously exciting and rewarding. And the best part? You'll never be alone. I'm right here in the trenches with you!

THE INCREDIBLE VANISHING WOMAN

The Incredible Vanishing Woman sounds vaguely like a failed circus sideshow act. (Failed because they kept losing track of her . . . "Wait, she was here a second ago . . .") But it could also describe many years in my life when I lost myself to the demands of others. Like so many women, my sense of self and my priorities took a backseat to everyone else's when I took on the very real responsibilities of adulthood. We're busy building careers, paying the mortgage, raising families, caring for aging parents, doing laundry, shopping for groceries, preparing meals, and on and on. When you look at it as a list of day-to-day responsibilities, losing oneself isn't all that hard to imagine in our amped-up, crazy-busy lives.

While I was in the throes of parenting small children and running a licensed day care in our home, there were months that went by when I didn't do a single thing that I could've called fun. Not one. When a rare couple of hours opened up and I had free time, I literally could not think of what to do. My mind would just go blank. I had spent so many years devoted to caring for the needs of others that I had no interests of my own. Not only that, but I had virtually no friends because I hadn't cultivated friendships. Oh, I had a friend or two who would invite me to play bunco (a dice game that is an excuse for women to drink a lot, as far as I can tell) or be part of a book club. They had their "girls' night out" and weekend get-aways, but I never went, deeming them unnecessary and self-ish. Instead, I tied my self-worth to being the best wife and mother I could possibly be, which in my mind meant tending to the needs of others.

It seems so sad to me now, but at the time I was running on fumes from dawn till dusk. Even sleep wasn't restorative; it was simply a physical necessity. There were no contemplative moments, no reflecting on life goals or personal ambitions. There was just a long list of things that needed to be done and other people's priorities.

I may have been the Incredible Vanishing Woman, but my problems—and my weight—were getting bigger and bigger.

What I see clearly now is that I lost my sense of self due to my own lack of boundaries and my inability to say no to the needs of others.

It wasn't just the responsibilities and obligations of my busy life that caused me to lose sight of who I was and my own sense of purpose. I lost my sense of self because, on some level, overempathizing with others' needs allowed me to ignore my own needs.

This may sound strange, but what I've come to realize is that many of us consummate people pleasers aren't just happy-go-lucky types who like to make other people happy. In my case, focusing on the needs of others was both a way to show the world that I was a good wife and devoted mother and a convenient way of stalling the hard work of confronting my own deep unhappiness. Deflecting attention away from myself seemed like a winning strategy; it gave me cover to avoid my problems while giving me validation from others that I was doing everything "right." I don't think it's just me either. Putting the needs of others first and doing everything "right" are powerful cultural messages that many of us cling to. And because I never do anything halfway, I swallowed this line of crap hook, line, and sinker.

What does any of this have to do with weight loss? you rightly ask. A lot, actually.

Focusing on the needs of others, working excessively, or overcommitting to volunteer activities—at the expense of our own health and happiness—is a self-inflicted wound. Nobody told me I couldn't hire a sitter every once in a while and go out with the girls. No one would've thought me selfish if I had dropped the kids at the gym's child care while I got in a workout.

No one, that is, except me.

It was what I now call the "demon dialogue" of self-doubt and self-criticism that I heard in my own head, and it kept me from leading a more balanced life for all those years. But eventually I was completely tapped out. In my case, I even came to resent the people in my own family, all of whom I love so deeply.

So how did I get the Incredible Vanishing Woman to reappear? Well, first I had to want to. The only thing that finally shook me out of my people-pleasing stupor was hitting rock bottom with my weight.

Learning to find time for things that I wanted to do— heck, figuring out *what* I wanted to do when I wasn't caring for everybody else all the time—took me a while to discover. When I asked myself that first critical question about what happiness would look like if I got to decide what it meant for myself, I realized that I had to start letting go of all the shoulds in my life that were holding me back.

THE "SHOULDS" SHACKLES

Recently, I was reading a piece written by syndicated columnist Leonard Pitts Jr. in which he reflects upon a different ending to the traditional "Snow White" fairy tale where, as we all know, she is awakened by true love's first kiss and then presumably lives happily ever after with her Prince Charming. In the new ending, Snow White is a beleaguered suburban mom with a babe in arms and a couple of other children clinging to her. Meanwhile her prince is asleep in the Barcalounger with ESPN blaring. Or something to that effect. This rendering of the fairy tale is Pitts's way of illustrating that in our accepted story line for a woman's life, the pinnacle of ambition is securing a husband (and by extension security), with no thought given to what comes after. While most of us would like to think that we've evolved beyond the stereotype, he points out that the endless stream of rom-com movies and the tabloid scrutiny of Hollywood starlets (though noticeably not their male counterparts) makes one wonder if maybe we have not advanced as much as we would hope.

Do we still cling to this idealized characterization of a "good girl"? Do we still send the message to our daughters that they have value only if they marry and have children? Well, I'm not here to psychoanalyze American culture or even Disney movies, but it's clear that societal messages about gender roles are still alive and well. Most of us accept these messages without really questioning them—we internalize them and then pass them along to our own children. Certainly, accepted customs are challenged and do change over time, but that change can be glacially slow. In the meantime we grow from children to adults, and raise our own children with much the same values that our parents instilled in us. Implicit in those messages that we internalize are a whole lot of shoulds.

Not all shoulds are bad, of course. What kind of world would we live in if we didn't adhere to most of our agreed-upon shoulds? I can think of a certain list of ten "thou shalt nots" that are a pretty potent set of laws to live by. What I'm talking about are the shoulds that may be holding us back. These are the expectations that we've internalized because we've been told we need to do these things to be a good person. I also refer to this concept as "playing by the rules of someone else's game." We never consciously agreed to these rules, but we've been holding ourselves accountable to them our entire adult lives. Not sure what I mean? Here are some examples of my shoulds:

- You should stay home with your children and raise them yourself.
- You should have a career and earn your own way in the world.
- You should have a clean, tidy home.
- You should go to church every Sunday.

- You should always enjoy spending time with your children and your spouse.
- You should be generous and giving, eager to please, and responsible.
- You should sit down to a home-cooked meal with your family every night.
- You should be selfless and put the needs of others ahead of your own.

WHEN I WAS FINALLY READY TO CHANGE MY HABITS FOREVER, MY APPROACH TO WEIGHT LOSS FELT DIFFERENT FROM HOW IT HAD BEFORE. THIS TIME IT WAS FOR MY REASONS ON MY TERMS.

None of these notions is bad in and of itself. In fact, you could certainly argue that these are all laudable aspirations, tried-and-true values to live by. But in my experience, I spent my entire adult life trying to define myself by many of these shoulds and found myself always coming up short, never measuring up to that list of ideals. Is this society's fault? No, but the fact that I swallowed them all without questioning their merits certainly didn't do me any favors. When you rely on external definitions, you give up the capacity to create your own identity. Ultimately, none of us can commit to health and wellness for the long term if we're clinging to false ideals. For me, those false ideals—those shoulds—shackled me, and they had to go.

When I was finally ready to commit to changing my eating habits forever, rather than suffering through yet another diet, my approach to weight loss felt different from how it had felt in any of my previous attempts. No longer was I desperately trying to lose weight because I despised how I looked and hated how I felt; I was doing it for my own health and happiness. My reasons, on my terms. I was moving toward something positive—a vision I had for my life. The burden of other people's judgment and of my own crushing self-criticism lifted, and I was free to soar as high as I could imagine. And I've found that I can imagine pretty high.

My "should" shackles are finally broken.

And what about all of those "should" messages that we may be passing along to our kids? My teenage son was working on a project for school a while back, and he had to come home and have a conversation with his dad and me about what we thought were the most important factors in raising children with high self-esteem. Without hesitation I answered, "unconditional love from your parents." To me, this means that the child doesn't have to *do* anything, doesn't have to *be* anything to earn a parent's love. The child is loved just because he or she *is*. No conditions, no qualifiers, no modifiers. This isn't to say that we don't want our kids to achieve all that they're capable of, because of course we do. We want them to excel and accomplish great things because of the satisfaction they experience, not because it is any kind of reflection on us or because it means they're "better" than their peers. No, the only shoulds that we ought to pass along to our kids are that they should take risks, they should discover their passions, and they should reach out to others both to learn from them and to mentor them. Likewise, we need to let them fail from time to time. Only in failure do we learn how resilient we are. I believe this is how we break the cycle of imposing an external standard of what's good enough onto our kids. They get to—*we* get to—define success for ourselves. Because that's the only standard of success that really matters.

Finding my authentic happiness is the happily ever after that gives me the courage to free myself from the "should" shackles. And as far as Snow White's storybook ending goes, maybe instead of just love's first kiss, she could've had a kick-ass job, a rockin' body, and a husband who helped a little more with the housework.

TIME VAMPIRES: THAT MASSIVE SUCKING SOUND

We value busyness in our culture. Ask people how they are, and as often as not you'll hear, "Busy!"

I do it myself all the time.

Well, we *are* busy! There are all of the regular responsibilities and obligations that we have to fulfill: going to work, taking care of our kids, and paying our bills. Then there are the fun but time-consuming things we want to do: exercising, watching sports, keeping up with friends, and entertaining. Your personal list may also include hobbies you love: sewing, reading, antique shopping, home-improvement projects, pickup softball games, volunteering as a Big Brother or Big Sister, or tinkering with an old '57 Cadillac you've got in a shed out back.

You may wonder what busyness has to do with digging out of emotional eating and learning to make yourself a priority. Well, it took me a long time to figure out that my hectic lifestyle was just as destructive to my health as my self-defeating eating habits. Slowly, I began to recognize that I had to free up time for my burgeoning healthy habits if I wanted a life that was more aligned with my newly established vision and goals.

As I began to unpack emotional eating it dawned on me that not only did my eating habits have to change, I had to rethink everything about how I scheduled and prioritized my time.

At the outset of my weight-loss journey my days (and nights . . . and weekends . . .) were jammed full of work responsibilities and family activities. There simply weren't big blocks of free time anywhere in my life to make room for anything new. So first off, I had to start chiseling out time in my packed planner each week for exercise, healthy meal planning, and food preparation. As I began to exercise I learned quickly that I would have to allow for adequate sleep each night too. It's hard enough to function properly when you're always running on empty, but when you add exercise to the mix your body really needs adequate rest and recovery. I set a goal to get in at least seven hours of quality sleep every night. That first year of weight loss involved a lot of fine-tuning as I scrutinized everything on my plate—my dinner plate *and* my schedule!

As I quickly learned, prioritizing healthy habits and making room for them every day is a learned skill; nobody is born with it. Certainly not me. So if you're not doing it as well as you'd like to be, don't sweat it. Old dogs may have a hard time learning new tricks, but we're not old dogs.

Having said that, you probably have some time vampires in your life; you know, the ones that suck up your valuable time without your really thinking about them. These are the gratuitous time wasters that fall considerably short of anybody's definition of *mandatory* or even *desirable*, landing somewhere around *passive default*. I offer up my own brain-dead activities: watching TV shows I've already seen before (*Seinfeld* doesn't count; it's been scientifically proven to get funnier each time you watch it), scrolling Facebook, and composing pithy tweets. TV and social media may be the most obvious targets, but think through how you're spending your downtime and assess whether or not you're really getting as much out of it as you could.

The big concern with these time wasters is that they can be a way of immersing ourselves in activities as a distraction from more important things. If a big problem (your weight) seems overwhelming, surfing Facebook is a convenient way of putting it on the back burner, so that there isn't time to deal with it. Coming to terms with this is all part of letting go of denial and raising self-awareness.

Whether it's at work or at play, we want to spend the twenty-four hours we're blessed with each day in a way that is directed and intentional. That kind of downtime is restorative and relaxing. You feel reenergized and you're ready to take on

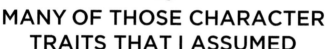

MANY OF THOSE CHARACTER TRAITS THAT I ASSUMED WERE ADMIRABLE—BEING SELFLESS, DEFERENTIAL, AND DUTIFUL—WERE THE VERY QUALITIES THAT MADE ME FAT.

the next task. We're all busy, right? But we need to zero in on those activities, people, and pastimes that bring us the deeply satisfying pleasure that we all crave.

BOUNDARIES, BABY!

When I look at this book in its entirety, it strikes me how every single strategy I've learned—really, *every single point* I make—is about putting yourself first. When you put yourself first you have high standards for yourself and your life. You expect to be happy and to have satisfying relationships with your family and friends, a job that is rewarding and fulfilling, time to pursue activities that bring you pleasure and joy, and the best possible health that you can achieve. You expect all of this, but you also know that you have to work for it. You are vigilant in your commitment to living well. That commitment means that you insist on the best of everything, not because you're arrogant or selfish, but because you deserve the very best: the best food you can afford, the best physical condition you can attain, the best doctors available to you, the best relationships you can build, the best mental state you can cultivate.

Putting yourself first may sound simple—and it is absolutely necessary to accomplish this transformation—but it's probably one of the hardest things I've ever had to do. It stands in complete opposition to everything that we've been taught, everything that we've assumed for most of our lives. We've always been told that we should put the needs of others ahead of our own. We should make do and be grateful for what we have. Well, that's all great just so long as we don't throw ourselves under the bus as a result. Unfortunately, many of those character traits that I assumed were admirable—being selfless, deferential, and dutiful—were the very qualities that made me fat. I sacrificed my own interests, needs, and desires because I thought that's what I was supposed to do.

Before I could start putting myself first, though, I had to figure out proper boundaries. Some people seem to do this effortlessly; I envy them. My Doormat No More! campaign was my first attempt at setting some limits on what I would and wouldn't do for others. Initially, I instituted this new policy for my kids, who, bless their little hearts, I'd trained to essentially take me for granted. I was their laundress and their chauffeur. I was deliverer of school lunches accidentally left at home and retriever of instruments absentmindedly forgotten on the band bus. One of my favorite Dr. Phil-isms (Dr. Phillip McGraw, of the TV show *Dr. Phil* fame) is that "you teach people how to treat you." So true! I'd taught my kids to treat me as if my time had no value. Their problems became my problems. In short, I had no boundaries. How in heaven's name was I ever gonna be able to put myself first if I had no boundaries?

Slowly, slowly, I started making changes. As I'll discuss in chapter nine, I started walking for exercise, but it was also a way to get out of the house and spend some time alone. I listened to music I enjoyed in the car instead of deferring to others. I cooked food that I looked forward to eating, not worrying about whether anybody else would like it. And eventually I began giving voice to the feelings—good and bad—that I'd always stuffed down before.

Boundaries become an issue in weight loss when we allow other people or activities to run roughshod over our own interests. These can be overt demands (take the insistent two-year-old banging on the bathroom door . . . no really, please take him—he's driving me nuts!) or the much more subtle passive activities that we fall into when we're too tired to see straight. They can be the volunteer organizations that are near and dear to our hearts, which rely on us too heavily simply because we're so damn dependable, or the hobbies we pursue because we enjoy them, but which leave us no time to plan healthy meals or exercise.

Learning to recognize boundaries and then set them appropriately was an important step in reclaiming myself. And having a sense of proper boundaries was absolutely vital before I could start to put myself first. Once I claimed ownership of my boundaries, I had a shot at turning things around.

WHAT IT MEANS TO PUT YOURSELF FIRST

I was watching a new TV show called *The Revolution* the week it premiered because it looked promising. It was about weight loss and transforming your life. Right up my alley. There was an expert in medicine (an MD), exercise (a personal trainer), emotional wellness (a psychologist), and fashion (the amazing Tim Gunn). The specialists were charged with helping the guest or guests (it was a pair of sisters the week I watched) in their area of expertise as they journeyed toward weight loss and explored facets of their lives that were holding them back. On one of the episodes I watched, the psychologist was talking to the guests about setting priorities and putting themselves first. To get the audience involved, she had them chant together with the guests, saying "NO!" when they were asked to do just one more thing for someone else. She shouted, "Just say," and the audience recited back with an uproarious, "NO!" Soon they were all in a frenzy yelling, "Just say no!!!" Hmmmm. That may work for television, but in real life it is much more complicated.

"Putting yourself first" may be used a lot in talking about weight loss, but almost never does anyone actually explain what this means or describe how to implement it in your life. Also, the consequences of putting yourself first can be extremely challenging, and it is one of the main reasons I believe many dieters fail. Is it absolutely necessary to put yourself first as you begin to transform your body and your life? I think we can agree you at least need to be in the top five on your to-do list. Prioritizing your needs will allow you to make room for healthy eating, exercise, pleasurable pursuits, and rewarding relationships. Maybe your needs won't be in the top five forever, but initially they will take time, energy, and laser-like focus. But let's be real: wanting to do it, knowing you need to do it, and *actually* doing it are entirely different. We're going to discuss some of the unexpected consequences of putting ourselves first later in the book (don't kid yourself; there will be pushback), but for now let's explore what it actually means to put yourself first.

Remember the time vampires? These are the passive activities that eat up our limited leisure time (television and the Internet are the two obvious ones). But there are also louder, more insistent vampires that exist in the form of the people and situations that intrude on our personal time. Back on the television show *The Revolution*, the psychologist who was leading the audience in that raucous version of "Just say no!" was addressing the people who actively try to recruit you to do things for them (e.g., "We need you to be PTA treasurer again because you've done such a great job the last two years . . . and nobody else will do it!"). But presumably she could also have been talking about other circumstances that can infringe on our time: for example, when a child procrastinates about completing his science fair project until the night before its due date, and *you* end up doing the project so he won't fail. The psychologist was absolutely correct; you are certainly within your right to "just say no" to these people and situations. But the big issues were never addressed on that show. Why are you saying no? How do you say no (and mean it)? Does it make you a bad person to say no? What's the fallout for saying no? How did I get myself into this frigging situation in the first place?!?

Let's take each of these examples—the PTA treasurer scenario, in which you're pressured to do the job again, and the procrastinating child who leaves you to scramble and pick up the pieces—and explore how to deal with them in a way that puts you first.

Imagine you're the busy working mom in our first scenario. When you were approached originally about being PTA treasurer you thought, *Oh sure, that would be a good way to make a contribution to my child's school. I'm a CPA, so it's a natural fit. And they've assured me it will only take a few hours a month.* So you sign on the dotted line. Some months it does only take a few hours of your time, but every couple of months there's a fundraiser that brings in hundreds of checks that must be recorded and deposited. There are taxes to do and other documentation that needs to be maintained, phone calls to return, and meetings to attend. And even though you're getting it all done, other priorities in your life are falling by the wayside so that you can meet your obligations in this role. At the end of the school year you breathe a sigh of relief, collect up the PTA treasurer's notebook, including all of the notes that you took on how to do this job effectively and efficiently, and go to drop them off with the president so that she can pass them along to next year's treasurer . . . and that's when she asks you to please do it again. And it's June, and it's sunny out, and you like her . . . and it really wasn't *that* much work, so you agree to do it for another year. But the next year it is a lot more work because the PTA decides to do a fundraising auction, and you get sucked in for many more hours of volunteering.

Meanwhile, your job is stressful, and your husband's job is demanding. You're both pulled in many different directions. The PTA role is just one of many demands on you, and maybe by itself it's not the ultimate cause of your increased stress, but it has definitely become a big responsibility and is causing you to push aside other activities. Like making a healthy dinner for your family on some weeknights. Like going to your favorite yoga class on Tuesday and Thursday evenings with your girlfriends. Like shopping at your favorite farmers' market on Saturdays. And on and on.

Now we come to that moment when you're being asked to do it again. For a third year. And they're desperate because no one else has volunteered to do it. You hesitate, because now you know how much work it is. But you've got it down and you are really good at it. You've got systems in place that make it easier and more efficient. You can probably do it better than anyone else could, so it seems only natural that you would do it again. But you remember how stressful it is when you're running straight from work to yet another meeting and how much you resent it when you don't have the time or energy to get to your exercise class or socialize with your friends. Are you going to do it again because people expect it of you, because it's easier to just do it and go along, or are you actually going to say aloud what that voice in your head is screaming: *No! It's time to pass the baton and let someone else do it. I'm paying too high a price for this, and I want more control over my free time.*

It's so easy to see the correct answer when it's someone else's life or, in this case, a hypothetical situation. We can see that she needs to graciously decline doing the job again so that she can regain some sanity and control in her life, and so that someone else has the opportunity to step up and learn the job. She needs to put herself first. Let's take a look at how she does that and the consequences of her doing so.

"We need you to be PTA treasurer again because you've done such a great job the last two years . . . and nobody else will do it!" was the plea in our scenario. When you're clear in your own mind that this is too great an infringement on your time, that you're paying too high a price for this responsibility, then it really requires no more than a simple, "No, I'm sorry, I can't" in response. End of discussion. Remember boundaries? Yep, this is them.

Does it make you a bad person to say no? Of course not. You may feel uncomfortable for a few moments, but, remarkably, most people will respect your boundaries when you assert them. And that's exactly what you're doing here. You're putting up a protective barrier around your time. When you create boundaries around your time, you give yourself permission to devote the time and energy to the people and activities that bring you pleasure and reinforce your commitment to wellness. The fallout from saying no in this particular scenario might be some feelings of guilt on your part, but honestly, in letting someone else pick up the mantle of responsibility for this task, you are making room for others to participate in leadership and community involvement. Pretty generous of you actually! So you deal with the fallout, the guilt, by putting it in perspective: *I am not the only person in the universe capable of doing this job. It got done before I came along, and it will continue to get done after someone else gets trained to do it.* Maybe you offer to help train that person so the transition goes smoothly. Guilt assuaged. Miracles do happen!

Next scenario: Your child has been dragging his feet for weeks about the science fair project that he needs to research, prepare, conduct, and complete. The two of you brainstormed some ideas for subjects, but nothing ever really sparked his interest, and he let it slide. Now it's the night before the project is due, and you're both panicked. Gone now are the potential topics of monitoring the development of mold on cheese or recording the growth of roots on a bean sprout. You need an experiment that can be conducted in ten minutes or less! You're angry with your child for procrastinating and leaving all of this for the eleventh hour; you're angry at yourself for forgetting about this looming deadline. You're resentful that you're going to be up past midnight tonight working on this damn science fair project, and you've got a presentation in the morning! So you drive to the store to get the poster board and scramble to pull something together, all the while vowing that you'll never let this happen again. After everyone else has gone to sleep you're finally done, and you stumble off to bed, exhausted. Tomorrow you'll be paying the price for another late night.

Not surprisingly, the next day you're totally wiped out. You're still upset about having to complete this project for your child, and you yell at him in the morning about how irresponsible he is. You both leave the house angry. You're so exhausted that you don't have the energy to make your lunch for work that day, and instead you end up grabbing a burger and fries later. At the end of the day there's just no way you've got the juice for your Wednesday night Zumba class. Not happening. You're getting the point here, aren't you? The negative impact of failing to put yourself first is far reaching.

Could you have said no to your child and let him bear the consequences for his failure to plan? Sure. Only you can decide

LEARNING TO PUT YOURSELF FIRST—AND MEAN IT—IS A FORM OF SELF-PROTECTION AND SELF-LOVE.

whether that's an option given the specific circumstances of the project, the age of the child, and the likely impact of your non-intervention. Why would you have said no? Because the darn kid should've taken care of this himself! You already passed sixth grade (or whatever grade he's in), remember?! Could you have sat down with him after the assignment was given to make sure that he had a project in mind? Yes. At that point, the two of you could have discussed any materials or supplies he needed and what kind of timeline he required in order to complete the assignment before the due date. All good ideas. Of course, children need to be shown how to succeed, as do we all. But let's say you did all of that, and Junior still failed to get the project underway until the night before. Does it make you a bad person to tell him no, you're not going to help him with it? I don't think so. Some parents may disagree. What's the fallout for your saying no? You'll have to evaluate those consequences based on the particulars of the situation and decide that on a case-by-case basis, but generally speaking, even if he fails the assignment—heck, even if he fails the class—it probably won't be a life-altering catastrophe. He'll probably still grow up to become a responsible, tax-paying citizen. If he learned anything from the experience, though, maybe when he's an adult he won't wait until April 14th to fill out his 1040.

I'm all too familiar with both of these scenarios, having been on several PTA executive boards and "supervised" more science fair projects than I can count. Pressure to put the needs of others ahead of our own can look like those insistent people compelling you to do something for them, or it can be a one-time project that comes at you from out of the blue and hijacks your plans. Or it can be the deeply engrained, habitual, unending duties that you've taken on as part of one of your many roles. These can be the hardest of all to recognize and root out. In most cases you sought out these roles (parent, spouse, employee), and you probably embraced the responsibilities that came with them. But some of us approach these tasks with a certain sense of self-sacrifice and self-importance that borders on martyrdom. When that happens, nobody wins.

Learning to put yourself first—and mean it—is a form of self-protection and self-love. When you value your time and

84

are realistic about your limits, you assert your own priorities and make it clear that you expect others to do the same. For those of us who were raised to value selflessness, this is a skill we need to develop. It's hard to do, but when we're secure in our right to claim it, doubt begins to fall away.

"I GET ONE DAMN SHOT AT LIFE AND I'M GOING TO LIVE IT TO ITS FULLEST EVERY DAY—NO REGRETS!"

When I made that all-important connection—that I wanted happiness for myself on my own terms for the rest of my life— it was an epiphany for me. Not the fact that I wanted to be happy, because, well, who doesn't want that? And yes, the "on my own terms" part was an epiphany, but that's not what I'm talking about here. What I'm talking about specifically is the "for the rest of my life" part.

The fact that it took me until my midforties to realize that I only get one shot at life is not really anything to brag about. It's not like I didn't realize that you only get one go-around. I guess when I was younger I just felt different about the passing of time. There always seemed to be so much time in front of me, you know? In my twenties and even my thirties I felt like I had so much of life yet to come. I was building a life and a family. I was immersed, certainly, and distracted with all of the crazy busyness that everyday life with a growing family entails. Like everyone else, we struggled to get ourselves established financially and make important career decisions. We bought a house, and then had a child or two (or four!), and then we bought a bigger house. In all of this busyness I guess I was blind to the fact that time was passing; I felt the urgency of pressing needs coming at me from every direction and gave almost no thought to the fact that my body was paying a price for the years of neglect. But I was young, right? I had my whole life ahead of me.

But slowly, in my forties, it began to dawn on me: *this really is the only life I get.* However much is still in front of me is all that there is! And the part that's left will feel different from the part I've already lived. I'll be older, maybe sicker, maybe fatter, maybe . . . I won't have as long as I want. That was a horrifying thought to me.

Later, after I'd lost weight and started running, this analogy occurred to me: When you're training for your first marathon you've maybe run a few half marathons, and you felt pretty good about them. You're filled with pride in your accomplishment. Thirteen-point-one miles is a long way, after all! When you decide you want to reach for the marathon, you begin to run farther. Your training runs go beyond the half-marathon distance, and you're routinely running fourteen, sixteen, up to twenty miles. It occurs to you that when you ran a half marathon, as exhausting and exhilarating as that was, that was the easy half! The second half is what separates the women from the girls. The second half is where endurance, stamina, perseverance, and mental strength come into play. In the second half, you find out what you're made of. You're more worn down; you've got to dig deep and give it everything you've got; and then, when you've done that, you give more. And maybe that's true for the second half of anything.

I have come to the conclusion that it's certainly true for the second half of my life.

I already lived the part where I could take my health for granted. I already lived the part where I could take my future for granted. The second half is where I'm going to have to dig deep if I want to make the most of this life. Now, without question, I'm a little slow on the uptake. You may very well have come to this realization at a much younger age than I did. I certainly hope so. But maybe you didn't. Maybe you're in your fifties or sixties and just recognizing that you've got to start taking better care of your body and your health. No matter what age you are when you come to this truth, the result is the same: you get the rest of your life, however long that may be, to work on it! And if you work at living your best, most authentic life every day, in terms of your physical health, your relationships, your job, and all of your activities, you will find that the second half—or however much you've got left on this earth—is the best half.

If you're overweight and unhappy about it, you may be tempted to regret choices that you've made up until now. I get that. But regret is a useless and destructive emotion. I have moments when I get so angry at myself for having "wasted" years of my life being fat, unhealthy, unhappy, and trying to live by someone else's measure of what was "good" and "worthy." Whether any of that anger and resentment is valid or not, what the hell purpose does it serve to regret it *now*? All that does is poison *this* moment. Why would I choose to do that? Well, I don't. Or at least I try not to. Because if I do, guess what? I've just wasted more time living in unhappiness, and I'll never get *this* moment ever again!

Maybe it's age, maybe it's a little bit of wisdom—Lord, let's hope so!—but I've learned that all of those shortcomings, all of those mistakes, and all of those bumps along the way have led me to this version of myself. I could not possibly have achieved all that I have if I hadn't first experienced each of the failures I endured on the way here.

While accepting my past is liberating, it doesn't let me off the hook. Every day I still have to focus on living authentically, challenging my underlying beliefs about myself, confronting what scares me, and pushing myself to the edge of my comfort zone. This can be intimidating, but it's also what keeps life interesting and, frankly, worth living. I've come to believe that being comfortable is overrated. Maybe what we should be reaching for is that knife-edge between what's safe

BEING COMFORTABLE
IS OVERRATED.

and what's not. Maybe fear and regret are the antithesis of personal growth and maturity. Maybe uncertainty about whether or not you're capable of doing something is okay; try it anyway. You never know. Maybe it won't be so scary if you go there with another brave soul. C'mon, take my hand! I'll go too!

Chapter Five

REACHING OUT: HAVING THE COURAGE TO ASK FOR HELP

Getting my head on straight about prioritizing healthy eating, setting appropriate boundaries, and claiming a little time for myself didn't come overnight. Though I knew that these lifestyle changes would maximize the chances that my lap-band could help me lose weight, I was still uncertain of exactly how to proceed in mapping out a new life.

When I reached out to the team at my weight-loss surgeon's office, I felt an immediate rapport with him and his staff. They really got it, on every level. They understood the pain and frustration of obesity. They were compassionate and understanding about my years of failure. They opened their arms with support and hope, standing at the ready to help me achieve my goals.

Knowing I had partners who had faith in my ability to succeed assured me that, in fact, I could. Weight loss had always seemed like only a vague hope before, no matter what method I tried. Even when I attended meetings or enlisted the help of a nutritionist or counselor of some kind, it always felt like I was in it alone. But here was a team of people who knew full well that I was capable of success.

This team approach felt so natural and supportive that when I stumbled upon it at my weight-loss surgeon's office I had a sort of "Duh!" smack-my-forehead moment.

I'd witnessed the power of teamwork before but hadn't ever adopted this approach myself. You see, my husband's political life started early in our marriage, when he was one of those eager young volunteers who stuffed envelopes, rang doorbells, and handed out flyers. Because he's bright and ambitious, he quickly became involved in political campaigns in a much more strategic way. By the time he was twenty-eight years old he was managing races for city council and eventually even a governor's race. But all of this was volunteer work that he did after putting in a full day of lawyering. At the ripe old age of thirty-three, in 1995, he became the candidate, running for—and winning—a seat on our county council. His passion was now his full-time job. Rob moved into the public life of an elected official, and the kids and I were right there with him.

Whether it was as a volunteer in the early days of his political career, or eventually as the candidate, Rob spent a lot of time working as part of a team on political campaigns. It was obvious to me that this type of team approach was vital to a campaign's success. There were field workers, finance experts, fundraising specialists, logistics people, schedulers, policy advisors, communications and media professionals, tech whizzes, and of course, an army of volunteers. Everybody on the team had the same goal, and each brought a unique expertise to the effort.

As I've said, political life brought with it a lot of stressors for our whole family, but they also taught me a thing or two about how to build a team and tackle a huge project. What I saw from my vantage point was that having a team of experienced and supportive people in place makes all the difference when you're trying to accomplish something monumental.

ASSEMBLING A TEAM

For years I had tried (and failed) to achieve weight loss on my own. I suppose it's our reverence for rugged individualism that leads to our belief that somehow you must do it alone or you didn't really earn it. But who accomplishes anything meaningful alone? Nobody! When it comes to weight loss, I think it was my fear that kept me quiet and isolated. I was afraid that telling people I wanted to lose weight meant acknowledging I was flawed and weak. And what if I told everyone I wanted to lose weight and then failed again? Each time I embarked on another weight-loss attempt I did it privately, anticipating the shame I would feel about failing . . . actually expecting to fail!

When I had my rock-bottom experience and decided I was done with failure, I moved forward with a sense of purpose. Initially, I was reluctant to tell people I had decided to have lap-band surgery, but by surrendering the idea that I had to accomplish weight loss alone, I was on my way to what was to become the deciding factor in my success: I was assembling a team.

In every sense, it felt as if a huge weight had been lifted off my shoulders. I could ask for help?!? This was a revelation to me! Ultimately, I learned that reaching out to others for help and support is critical to success. The beauty of it is that now I am in a position to do that for others, but before I get to that, let me introduce you to my team and tell you how I came to find them all, and how each one has helped me.

Go, team!

FAMILY

When I decided I was ready to change my life I knew I needed support from the person I had the closest relationship with: my husband. My decision to have lap-band surgery worried him initially; the surgical risks are not insignificant, and the cost was a strain on our already maxed-out budget. But when I explained how important the surgery was to my getting better, and he could see that I was committed to doing everything I could to be successful, he backed me 100 percent. We faced my surgery, my recovery, and everything that I needed to change about my lifestyle together, as a united front.

My kids were also completely supportive of the changes that I needed to make. Initially, my cooking habits didn't change much, but as I lost weight I gradually started cooking with healthier ingredients. Ground turkey rather than beef (now I make buffalo and even elk burgers!), quinoa instead of rice, and kale as an occasional alternative to leaf lettuce. Some of my kids are more aligned with my eating habits than others, but most important, they supported me when I needed them most.

A while ago I was on a "patient success stories" panel at the clinic where I had my lap-band surgery. We were each asked to describe how our families reacted to our decision to lose weight. I went first and reported what I just told you: that my family was incredibly supportive, even though sometimes it's been difficult for them because I'm busy working out or am just not as available as I once was. They're proud of me, and I feel their love and encouragement daily.

"Well, that's great, but it's not all rainbows and unicorns for the rest of us, is it?" the facilitator said to the audience. She went on to talk about how some people have pushback from family members. Children may complain about different foods showing up on the dinner table; spouses may grumble about not having their favorite ice cream in the house. Worse, they may try to manipulate or derail their loved one's weight-loss efforts.

Despite the harshness of her comment, I could see there was truth to what she said. Not everyone has a "rainbows and unicorns" kind of experience when they try to enlist their family's help in their weight loss. In their defense, these family members may not even be aware that they're undermining their loved one's success. But the facilitator's point was that we're the ones who must be alert to sabotage by others so that we won't fall into the trap and abandon our goals just to keep the peace. She's absolutely right about that.

I hear from people all the time whose husbands cook unhealthy meals, even though they know their wife is trying to lose weight. Or a girlfriend offers to treat for brunch at their favorite guilty-pleasure cafe, tempting with mile-high pancakes and mimosas. Ugh, this stuff is so hard to resist, isn't it?

But the more important question is why someone who loves you would act in a way that completely disregards your stated wishes. If you're clear in your goal to make better food choices, exercise, lose weight, and live healthier, why would a loved one do anything other than support that effort? I think you already know the answer to that question: they have some reason why they don't want you to succeed. Again, they may not be conscious of it, but your decision to change may feel threatening to them. They may be afraid that if you become fit and healthy you might leave. Or perhaps they feel defensive because your decision to live healthier stands as a challenge to their own bad habits.

A very important part of my journey has been learning to advocate for myself. It's more than just learning how to put yourself at the top of your own to-do list. It's tuning in to what you really need to be happy and satisfied, and then going after it with everything you've got. I'm so fortunate that my family is totally on the same page with that. If they weren't, I'd have to bash 'em over the head or something, but if your family isn't, try a gentler approach than that. It's possible that their own fears and anxieties get in the way of their wholehearted support of your goals. Be sensitive to those insecurities by reassuring them that you're eating healthy, exercising, and losing weight so that you'll feel better, and that doing so means you'll be around for many more years. Those years will be happier too, and isn't that ultimately what they want for you?

If you're able to negotiate a new normal with your family members on your own, then great! If you feel a lot of push and pull from them as you all stumble along this new path, consider enlisting the support of a professional therapist who can help you find ways to balance everyone's needs and concerns. Experiencing resistance from your spouse or kids (or both!) is perfectly normal. I'm betting that they'll be on your A-team eventually, but if they aren't right away, you may need some counseling to understand and address the pushback so you can become more aligned.

Back at my house, we're still negotiating the details of Mom's new life. We're far from perfect, but our family unit is strong, and we have each other's backs. My husband and kids are my biggest cheerleaders and my soft place to land. They know all my baggage, and for some reason they love me anyway. When I assembled my team, they were my first-round draft pick.

FRIENDS

If you're lucky enough to live in the same town you grew up in, you may have friends you've known your entire life. I've moved more times than I can count and have lost track of nearly everyone I knew before I was in high school. I count many high school and college friends among my closest, but as I mentioned before, there were years in my life that I was so wrapped up in raising my children that I neglected my friendships to the point where I had almost no friends I saw with any frequency. I am forever indebted to those intrepid souls who hung in there with me through those years, but I think I pushed those relationships aside because they just didn't have the urgency that the needs of my young children did. I have also come to realize that I subconsciously withdrew from social activities because I was so uncomfortable with my weight, even around my closest friends.

The children were my built-in excuse for not attending political or social functions with my husband, but the truth is that I was embarrassed to be seen by nearly anyone. In the few photos that exist of me at my heaviest (ask anybody who's ever been obese—they'll tell you they avoid being photographed like the plague) I see the humiliation in my own eyes. I felt I needed to apologize for taking up space. It's a horribly painful way to live, so I withdrew.

As I got bigger, my world got smaller.

I found that as I started losing weight, as I started feeling better, I started reaching out more to my longtime friends and to new friends. And as my world opened up in new directions, it expanded to include an entirely new group of friends. I met them at yoga or in the locker room at the Y. I met them through a mutual friend or on social media. They may not all turn out to be lifelong friends, but they are interesting people whose insight and perspective I find fascinating. The one thing they all have in common is that they are living lives filled with passion. From them I've learned to push beyond my comfort zone, to explore my own untapped potential and unleash my own passions.

AS I GOT BIGGER, MY WORLD GOT SMALLER.

Now I'm one of those silly saps who walks around saying things like, "A stranger is just a friend you haven't met yet." And other such corny clichés. I find myself drawn to people who have struggled, yet have somehow persevered. They have interesting stories to tell, and they're not afraid to share them. They have taught me that making human connections and supporting one another is ultimately what we're all here to do on this earth.

My longtime friends will always be an important part of my support team, but I've found that there's a great big world out there full of new friends who I also want in my corner.

HEALTH CARE TEAM

The general practitioner who so quickly dismissed my idea of having lap-band surgery wasn't the only doctor who didn't offer a sympathetic approach to my weight issues. More than a decade before that appointment I was seeing a different doctor about some ailment or another, and I decided to ask him about my weight issue. I was at least seventy-five pounds overweight at the time. During the final minutes of my appointment I asked him if he had any advice for me about my weight. What could I do to lose weight? I was worried about my health, and I was very unhappy. He said, and I can still quote him all these years later because I remember his response verbatim, "Yes, you really need to get that under control, because it's only going to get harder to lose weight the older you get." And then he walked out. Gee, thanks. That was helpful . . . *not!*

Doctors are our trusted advisors. We rely on them to care for us when we're sick and to guide our health decisions throughout our lives. They can be a source of information and assurance, or they can rush in and out of the examining room, busy with their own thoughts and schedules, offering platitudes and shutting down our inquiries with scarcely a look up from their clipboard.

These days I have a handful of very helpful doctors who I count on to help keep me healthy. My lap-band doctor, for example, has made time to meet with me even when I had no pressing medical concern but did have questions about my band and my weight-loss experience. Everyone on his team has been similarly helpful and supportive. Many of the staff have bands or have undergone some other form of bariatric surgery, so they understand patients' concerns firsthand. It's worth noting that as a part of their screening process, each patient sees a psychologist who is trained in obesity and body image. They're screening for people whose expectation of surgery may be unrealistic, setting them up for failure and disappointment.

Among the other doctors on my team are an orthopedic surgeon who had to give me the bad news that I have advanced osteoarthritis (I had knee surgery in 2012 to repair what he could salvage of my shredded cartilage), a naturopath I sought out when I was experiencing severe menopause symptoms, various physical therapists, a chiropractor, and even an acupuncturist! I've done body composition scans, massage therapy, and cosmetic surgery too (I had excess skin removed around my abdomen). And as I mentioned in chapter two, I saw a therapist for a time to help me sort out the residual childhood trauma I experienced and the complicated feelings that led to my emotional eating. Additionally, Rob and I went through couples counseling to help us face and change some of the destructive habits that caused me to push my feelings away rather than share them with him. After years of sublimating my needs, I needed help learning how to assert myself in a positive, effective way. The resentment and bitterness I felt needed a constructive outlet and a voice. In counseling, we each owned up to our parts in the mistakes we made, and we found a new way of communicating. There is no doubt in my mind that both individual and marriage counseling played an important role in my healing.

I will say, without reservation, I could not have achieved the weight-loss success that I have without this cadre of healthcare professionals to help me. I've learned to find practitioners who are willing to work with me when I have a problem, and to figure out a plan of action together. As you move forward in your own journey, I encourage you to assemble a team of professionals who take the time to know you, to listen to you, and to respond thoughtfully to your questions and concerns.

Doctors are on the front lines of the obesity issue every day. They have an opportunity—I would say an obligation—like no one else we come into contact with to approach this sensitive topic in a way that offers help and hope to their patients. But they need to take the time to really listen to their patients' concerns and help find workable solutions. Doctors, I hope you're listening.

TEACHERS

Of course everybody we run into in the course of our lives has something to teach us, but the teachers I'm talking about here are the instructors, coaches, and trainers who have been instrumental in my transformation. Some of them were people I met through structured settings, like exercise classes, while others were just ordinary folks who became mentors to me.

As I'll explain in chapter nine, I didn't begin exercising immediately when I started losing weight. Though I started walking not long after my lap-band surgery, I was fully two years into my journey before I began running. Less than six months after that I had my first bona fide injury in the form of a stress fracture.

Desperate to find an alternative workout, I had several friends and a chiropractor suggest hot yoga to me. Being ever-so-slightly stubborn (ahem), I pooh-poohed it, thinking it wasn't "real" exercise (not to mention it was all just a little

YOGA HEALED ME, BODY AND SOUL.

too woo-woo for me). But I had few options at that point, so a friend dragged me to a Bikram hot-yoga class. I didn't fully understand why at the time, but the class's structure, intensity, and rhythm really resonated with me. I'm always cold, so

I craved the heat. I loved the fact that the ninety-minute class was exactly the same twenty-six poses (each done twice) every single class—the only thing that was different from class to class was me. That is, my body. I learned to really tune in to how I felt on any given day. Were my muscles sore from the previous day's workout? I learned to be patient with myself. Improvement comes quickly at first, but then gains can be glacially slow. These and so many other lessons I learned in that hot room I now apply to all areas of my life. Among those lessons was to stop comparing myself to other people. In class we're taught to look at ourselves in the mirror with a fixed focus, because that focus aids balance. Lose your focus—look away—and you will fall. This is a great metaphor for everything having to do with healthy living. There is no denial in that room. You cannot look away from your own reality. You feel the presence of everyone else in the room, but their individual movements do not break your concentration.

The men and women who lead this yoga practice are highly trained, but they're also just profoundly accepting and compassionate people. Personally, I'm convinced that there's a special place in heaven for yoga instructors. One of my favorite instructors reminds us frequently that we need to be "comfortable being uncomfortable." Truer words were never spoken.

Even though being fat was uncomfortable, I felt safe—in a way—inside that comfort zone. Yoga healed me, body and soul.

In addition to my wonderful yogis, I count many others as my teachers in health and wellness. I work with a personal trainer whom I adore. She is compassionate but never indulges my grumbling. She seems to know exactly how far to push me without breaking me. I've not only gained physical strength this way, but I'm also a lot tougher mentally because she's helped me discover what I'm capable of.

Other teachers include experts in nutrition, food safety, and emotional eating, whose websites and blogs are now a part of my daily reading. But my teachers are also the people I meet in the course of normal life—everyday people who are passionate about running, cycling, or some other aspect of healthy living. Many have had transformative experiences of their own; I've had profound discussions with people who broke free from addictions to alcohol and drugs. Each of these people has taught me to be open to the wisdom we all hold. My teachers, then, are everyone—anyone—who is willing to share a little bit of that wisdom with me.

AUXILIARY TEAM

My auxiliary team is a sort of secondary support team that I call in for backup and assistance with some of my ancillary goals for healthy living. These are the "feel good" team members who help me feel more confident walking through the world. They're not absolutely necessary, but using them is a constant reminder of that revelatory thought I had when my world came crashing down around me: *I am worth the time, effort, and money it will take to get better.*

Obviously, when I was losing weight I had to change wardrobes several times. While dropping sizes, I shopped at thrift and consignment stores, in addition to discount retailers. Weight comes off in unexpected places, so not only did my wardrobe change several times, I also went down a full shoe size! Once I was confident that my weight had stabilized, I hired a personal stylist to help me weed through the remainder of those thrift and consignment store finds and begin to build a wardrobe for my new body and my new life. She took my measurements and evaluated my body shape; then we talked style. With her help I chose a personal style (sort of a vintage-glamour-meets-modern-casual look) that I now keep in mind every time I'm out shopping. Her advice has already stopped me from falling back into my fashion comfort zone, encouraging me instead to reach for a professional yet fresh look. Hiring a stylist wasn't cheap, but I consider it an investment in my new look and my new life.

Of course, looking our best is about much more than clothing. I dyed my own hair for years, but after having colored it raspberry one too many times, I gave up and started getting it done in a salon. Oh, I know I can buy a box of hair color for about eight dollars, and it can cost ten times that much to get it done in a salon, but considering my hair-coloring skills, the salon color looks at least ten times better. Only you can decide if that expenditure is in the cards for you, but for me it's worth the cost because I don't have to worry about my hair looking like a color of sherbet.

Then there are the countless other things we do to look and feel good: manicures, pedicures, waxing, massages, and so on. Again, only you can decide how much of this your budget will allow, but always shortchanging yourself of the little luxuries in life will only leave you feeling like you don't matter. When you *feel* like you don't matter, you tend to *act* like you don't matter, which leads to—you guessed it—shortchanging your eating and exercise goals. Treating yourself like you matter, like you would treat your very best friend or a beloved sister, is affirmation that you deserve the time and attention that it takes to feel good.

Having said all of that, it's certainly possible to go overboard and spend too much time worrying about the way you look. After all, what we really want is to *feel* our best. So there's something to be said for not always worrying about how I look. When I'm headed out for a run, I've got the appropriate gear, but I certainly don't worry about my hair and makeup. And when I'm diving into the pool, I've got a good set of goggles and a swim cap, but I'm not worried about what my hair is gonna look like afterward.

But because I'm a girl and sometimes it *does* matter, every once in a while I like to pull out all the stops and really look good. When I do, the best reward is that, because of all the hard work I put in, I feel amazing!

OUR TEAM MANTRA

Whether you're a cyclist or not, you're probably familiar with the concept of "drafting." The physics of it are such that the leader creates a "draft zone" behind him or her; another cyclist pulling into this space will benefit from the pull created in this wake, and the person will need to expend less effort to maintain the same speed as the leader. Interestingly, there is a measureable benefit for the leader as well. It is a perfect symbiotic relationship. More on the benefit to the leader in chapter eleven.

THERE IS NO "RIGHT WAY" OR "WRONG WAY" TO LOSE WEIGHT.

What I've learned through my transformation is that weight loss is a similar road. Rather than travel the road alone— something I struggled to do for more than twenty years prior to my weight-loss success, expending maximum effort yet coming up short every time—I learned to ride with a team.

Surrendering the idea that I had to do this alone—that somehow going it alone was more virtuous—was critical. From that first timid call to the weight-loss surgical center to seeking out advice from new friends about the best way to train for a marathon, I've learned that reaching out and asking for help is key. Now I know the magic of drafting with a team. When I meet someone who has important knowledge I need to succeed, or someone who's a little ahead of me on the path, I pull in behind. I ask questions, I take notes, and I emulate what they're doing. I let them help me.

As I said before, it's an illusion to think that anybody accomplishes anything meaningful alone. Furthermore, there is no "right way" or "wrong way" to lose weight. And there is certainly no limit to the number of people you may want on your team. Whether it's in fitness or in weight loss, we all do better when we support one another. Never be afraid to ask for help; before you know it, people will be pulling in behind you to draft in your wake!

Chapter Six

CREATING A FOOD SANCTUARY IN MY LIFE: REMAKING THE FAMILY FOOD CULTURE

inally!" the readers exclaim in unison. "She's gonna get to the point about what to eat, how to eat, and how to actually lose weight!"

Oh, don't get your panties in a bunch. Of course I was gonna get to it, but you can't just jump in at this point without laying the proper groundwork. How do I know that? Because that's exactly what I used to do every time I started a new diet! In fact, most diets start by throwing down lots of rules about what you can and can't eat on their plan and offering up meal plans, recipes, and grocery shopping lists. Yet none of that stuff means anything if you haven't got a solid foundation to build on and a clear understanding of why this is important to you. *You must believe at your core that you deserve something better for yourself, and that "something better" is losing weight and improving your health.* Otherwise, you're just trying desperately to follow somebody else's rules again, like every other time you have dieted. For weight loss to be long lasting, your new habits and behaviors must be aligned with your lifestyle and values. You must understand your own motivations and be willing to come up with strategies that play to your strengths and manage your weaknesses. At the risk of sounding immodest, this is exactly why I have succeeded where many fail. I am brutally honest with myself about what I can realistically do. When I stopped relying on diet experts' opinions about what *should* work and figured out for myself what actually *does* work . . . I succeeded.

YOU ALREADY KNOW THAT CHEETOS ARE BAD AND BROCCOLI IS GOOD.

This chapter and the next two are a rundown of the healthy eating strategies and principles that I used to help me lose 120 pounds and keep them off for more than eight years. The strategies and principles reflect my lifestyle and my values. They are as unique to me as my fingerprints, but I encourage you to try them because, based on my own experience and what I have heard from many others, I believe they solve some of the most common problems we run up against in healthy eating.

While you're reading, keep these four things in mind:

1. These are everyday working strategies for incorporating healthy habits into your life. It is not a list of

foods to eat or a shopping list. You already know that Cheetos are bad and broccoli is good.

2. The strategies work no matter how much weight you want to lose, how much money you have, how old you are, or how busy you are. Forgive a little tough love here, but every time you hear yourself muttering, "Oh, that's easy for her to say—she doesn't have _____," whatever's in that blank space is an excuse. I've heard 'em all. Heck, I've said 'em all! Resting on excuses will get you nowhere.

3. While this isn't a diet—you're developing an eating plan for life—I suggest you use a program for structure and support. It can be a formal program (I like Weight Watchers a lot), it can be a food-tracker app (I like Fooducate and MyFitnessPal), it can be weight-loss surgery, or any of a number of other well-tested plans.

4. This process is all about creating change. In order to succeed you must embrace it. You must revel in it. If you resist it, gritting your teeth, cursing me under your breath, you will hate it. If you hate it, you will fail.

Transformational behavioral change isn't just a paradigm shift; it's a thousand paradigm shifts. And the biggest shift of all? "This is the best thing that could possibly be happening to me right now, and I can't wait to get out there and start creating my new life!"

Let's go get it!

UNHEALTHY FOOD DOES NOT CROSS MY THRESHOLD

When I came up against challenges as I was losing weight, I would break the obstacle down into its elements. As I noodled the problem, asking myself things like, *What was I doing when this or that happened?* and *What was I feeling when those anxious feelings started to creep up?*, pictures would pop into my head. You see, I'm a very visual person. Over time I consciously developed these pictures into visual cues to keep me focused on what I wanted to accomplish. In doing so, the issue became more concrete, and I could "see" the solution. When I talked earlier about playing to my strengths, this is exactly what I meant.

I PLAY TO MY STRENGTHS AND MANAGE MY WEAKNESSES.

For example, in my mind, I visualize my house. Each of the doors is a point of entry, a threshold. We have dead-bolt locks and a security system to keep out those who would do us harm. Because of those measures, my loved ones and I are protected within its walls. Our home is our safe haven, our sanctuary. When we're out in the world we must accommodate others and put on our game face in order to deal with the challenges of the day, but at home we can let our guard down.

When it came to food, my home wasn't always a safe haven. For years I allowed unhealthy food into our house, justifying it by telling myself that the "kid-friendly" foods I bought (chicken nuggets, frozen waffles, toaster pastries) were what the kids wanted and made them happy. I bought chips, cinnamon rolls, nachos fixin's, and other treats for my husband, rationalizing that, since he enjoyed them occasionally, my buying them was proof of how much I loved him. All the while I knew that I would eat (more than) my share of all this garbage, but what

EAT LIKE IT MATTERS

was I to do? Should I deny my family the right to have their favorite foods simply because I was unable to control myself? Why should they be denied all their favorites just because I have this weakness? Naturally, all of this was going on amid my many attempts at weight loss.

It seems obvious to me now, but I was using my guilt over "denying" my family certain foods as a cover to indulge in a behavior that, despite my protestations that I wanted to lose weight, I really didn't want to give up or even acknowledge. (Do you hear the denial?) I knew in my heart of hearts that I couldn't control myself in the face of these foods when I was feeling overwhelmed or vulnerable. I knew that when I couldn't cope I would turn to those very foods as a pressure relief valve. And when those foods were in my house and I was dieting? Man, oh man, there wasn't a chance in the world I was going to succeed! I used to say that I could do everything right for twenty-three hours and fifty minutes of the day and then blow it all in ten minutes. Five minutes, on a bad day!

But what I came to realize is that it's okay for me to keep those temptations on the other side of my threshold. When I set aside the denial, the guilt, and the judgment (questions like, *Am I a bad mom for "denying" this stuff to my family?*, *Why can't I just control myself?*, and, *Why can't I do "everything in moderation" as we're told constantly by the so-called diet experts?*), I decided that I had the right to ask for an environment that was safe for everybody in our household, including me. Look, if we had a family member who was allergic to peanuts, we certainly wouldn't think twice about banning all nut products from our household, would we? We would consider it a safety issue.

For me, this is a safety issue. I am protecting myself from myself, if you will. When I am completely honest with myself I know that I still have issues with food! Heck, if there was a quart of Ben & Jerry's Chunky Monkey in the freezer, it would be calling to me at 2:00 a.m. (yes, I can hear it all the way upstairs). Removing the opportunity to indulge is just so much easier than trying to white-knuckle it out and rely on willpower. And even though I am a normal weight now, I will probably never be "cured" of my propensity to turn to food when I feel anxious or overwhelmed. The best I can hope for is to be conscious of this tendency and to manage it.

I play to my strengths and manage my weaknesses.

I no longer feel guilty about my "no unhealthy food crosses my threshold" rule depriving my family. Instead, having learned to tune in to my own needs, to be honest about my habits (I still eat sometimes when I'm upset, but now I do it with strawberries!), and to advocate for what I need, I have created that safe haven in my home that I envisioned. Now my home is a sanctuary where the only food choices to be made are good ones.

THE FORCE FIELD

Creating a safe haven in our homes is all well and good, but what about the rest of our day—*most* of our day? When we're out in the wild and woolly world of work, school, the mall, the airport, and all the other places we have to be in our busy lives? Once we cross our own threshold, how do we deal with the onslaught of unhealthy food on nearly every street corner?

Dammit Jim, I'm a doctor, not a registered dietician!

(I'm a Trekkie from waaaaaaay back, so bear with me for a sec.)

Again, here's a visual cue to make a rather abstract concept more concrete: imagine a force field (hence the *Star Trek* reference). When I'm confronted with the sights and smells of enticing food out in the real world, I literally picture an invisible force field forming a protective barrier between me and those seductive aromas. Just like the principle that unhealthy food does not cross my threshold, the evil food's siren song cannot penetrate the force field. (I'm jumping ahead of myself here, but will soon get to the Some Foods Are Truly Evil principle.)

It may sound silly, but it's a strategy that really works. Rather than allowing myself to be manipulated by the tantalizing sights and smells, I create mindfulness, which reinforces my goals and my faith in myself to outwit such temptations. Again, this isn't willpower, it's skill-power! It's a way of building confidence in your own capacity to outmaneuver temptation. I call it "exercising my self-care muscles," and just like with any kind of exercise, the more you do it, the stronger those muscles get!

I'm kind of a stubborn old broad, and I don't like to be manipulated by the advertising and marketing forces trying to separate me from my good health. It drives me just a little bit bonkers that we are told constantly that we deserve to indulge in fattening culinary abominations because we work hard. So what? Everybody works hard; we're all busy and stressed out. Eating a crappy diet is not going to make you feel better; in fact, quite the opposite is true. But you've got to be willing to tune out those voices and listen carefully to your own voice. Be willing to see that a long, healthy life is more of a treat than a quadruple-venti-white-chocolate-peppermint mocha (with whip) could ever be.

All of these treats and exceptions that we make can add up to a whole lot of high-calorie, unplanned, ad hoc eating. This is the death knell of weight loss and healthy living. When you have an eating plan in place—you've packed a lunch and have healthy snacks prepped and ready to go *before you race out the door in the morning*—you're much less likely to succumb to the impulsive treats that tempt us at every turn.

So put up your force field, exercise your self-care muscles, *Get Smart*, and drop the Cone of Silence over yourself to block out the nonsense. (And yes, I really did just reference another 1960s TV show.)

SOME FOODS ARE TRULY EVIL

First, let me say that food snobs used to annoy the crap outta me. I pictured them shopping at farmers' markets and buying artisanal cheese made from pastured, organic cows, spending a small fortune on their weekly groceries, and it seemed like they thought the rest of us were unenlightened schmucks for not following their lead. I imagined them turning up their noses at the more pedestrian mass-market grocery stores that the proletariat (read: the rest of us) shop in.

Oh brother, do these people have nothing else to do? I'd think to myself.

I, on the other hand, am cheap and practical. Out of necessity, I've had to be. I have four kids and a husband who need to be fed on a regular basis. Having lots of mouths to feed and not a lot of money to do it meant that for most of my adult life I've been a coupon-clipping, casserole-making maven. Plus, I'm busy! I don't have time to drive all over town looking for specialty ingredients and paying top dollar for them. I always say, "If it can't be found at Safeway, it's just not happening at my house!"

While all of that is still true, a funny thing happened when I started losing weight. I started reading. (About food, I mean. I've actually been able to read for quite some time.) I started reading books about food quality and what's going on inside our bodies when we eat. I became interested in why certain foods were triggers for me to overeat and why I seemed so powerless around them. What I learned became one of the biggest paradigm shifts I have undergone with regard to food. That paradigm shift?

I have come to the conclusion that some foods are truly evil.

I HAVE COME TO THE CONCLUSION THAT SOME FOODS ARE TRULY EVIL.

It's not the foods' fault, of course. There are armies of food scientists, chemical engineers, and other nefarious types in lab coats clandestinely working to develop irresistible combinations of taste, smell, and mouthfeel. These delectable combinations are then manufactured into a total sensory experience that we're invited to buy in grocery stores, chain restaurants, fast-food outlets, convenience stores, and coffee houses across America. To say that this stuff is heavily marketed is a gross understatement. The "best" of them become cultural icons (pumpkin spice latte, anyone?). Their appeal transcends the food's taste and becomes part of a lifestyle. Wow, that's some impressive marketing.

And this stuff tastes good, right? Whether it's a seasonal coffee drink, an ooey-gooey cinnamon roll in the mall food court, or a Southern Smokehouse Bacon Burger with ancho BBQ at Chili's (with fries, it has 2,290 calories, 139 grams of fat, and 271 percent of the daily recommend allowance of sodium), this stuff blasts our senses on every level, leaving us weak in the knees and begging for more.

What I started learning from my reading was that these hyperpalatable foods set off explosions of feel-good chemical reactions in our brains. They draw us in by first seducing us with their tantalizing smells and appealing visual cues (really, the pulling of cheese should be considered pornographic), and then they snare us with layer upon layer of different textures and flavors. And then the real fun begins. Our brains light up like pinball machines as they're flooded with the chemicals produced when we eat these culinary wonders.

Two fellows who are much smarter than me looked at the way these foods hijack our brain chemistry and explain why we end up at the mercy of the seemingly endless variety of these diabolical food combinations. In *The End of Overeating: Taking Control of the Insatiable American Appetite*, the former FDA commissioner who took on the tobacco industry, Dr. David A. Kessler, explains how "conditioned hypereating" becomes a normal behavior for many whose natural appetite self-regulators get short-circuited. In *Salt Sugar Fat: How the Food Giants Hooked Us*, *New York Times* reporter Michael Moss reveals the deliberate and insidious actions the food industry has taken to build a processed-food empire at the expense of public health. Food manufacturers use salt, sugar, and fat to achieve what Moss refers to as the perfect "bliss point." The bliss point is a way food scientists quantify the perfect balance of craving, taste, and irresistibility. They can literally manipulate the sensory intensity of any given processed food. It's almost as if our free will is being engineered right out of our brains.

This is some scary shit.

Can I just say, I am a cantankerous old broad. When I learned this—well, I'm just gonna say it—I was pissed! I do not like being played for a fool. I stopped eating at chain restaurants and buying most processed foods at that point. I don't intend on rewarding that type of corporate behavior by giving them any of my money. They certainly have the right to sell it, but likewise I have the right not to buy it.

There are other compelling arguments, beyond weight loss, for avoiding processed foods. This stuff is a chemical soup of bad-for-you ingredients. Preservatives, food colorings, artificial flavors, and even "natural" flavors can contain a whole lot of things you would never put on your plate if you could see them. And then there is the whole debate about GMOs (genetically modified organisms). Plants and animals can be genetically altered to have a specific characteristic of another plant or animal by introducing the genetic material of one into the cell wall of another. Typically, this is done to make the plant, for example, become more resistant to certain insects, or to supposedly boost its nutrition.

To date, the science around genetic engineering is controversial and inconclusive, but it's important to note that some of the most common agricultural products in the US—corn, soybeans, rapeseed (the raw material used to make canola oil)—are routinely genetically modified. (One source for further information about all of this is the Non-GMO Project's website.) Opponents of this practice cite cases of increased allergic reactions and other unknown health risks to the general public as reason enough why foods containing GMOs ought to be labeled as such. Labeling laws may change in the future, but in the meantime, if this is important to you, buy organic. Organic foods cannot be genetically altered, nor can animals whose meat or milk is sold as organic be fed a diet containing GMOs.

Honestly, it's enough to make me want to start wearing Birkenstocks and growing all my own food.

Still, there are two important things to remember about all of this before we resort to going off the grid. First, there are plenty of people who regularly dine at chain restaurants and eat a diet containing processed foods and GMOs who don't have a weight problem. Are they just genetically luckier than us? Could be. Maybe some of us are more affected by the feel-good chemicals that flood our brains when we eat sugar (for example) than others. Maybe some of us are more susceptible to cell mutations brought on by environmental and dietary agents. Fair or not, that's the nature of humanity: we're all different.

IT'S EASY TO BECOME OVER-WHELMED BY THE FLOOD OF INFORMATION AVAILABLE AND THEN TRY TO PURGE ALL "BAD" FOODS FROM YOUR DIET.

And second, though I now eat a diet that is almost completely devoid of processed foods and I don't patronize establishments that serve the kinds of hyperpalatable foods I described above, I didn't start my weight-loss journey eating that way. In fact, the only thing I did differently was eat less. Am I much healthier now because I don't eat that stuff? Yes, undoubtedly. Do I sleep better at night and have more energy, clearer skin, fewer food cravings, and fewer gastrointestinal problems? Yes, absolutely. But I don't weigh less because of it.

I encourage you to learn more about food safety, brain chemistry, and what's going on inside your own body, but don't let all of that information become an impediment to weight loss. It's easy to become overwhelmed by the flood of information available and then try to purge all "bad" foods from your diet, only to become frustrated with how difficult that is to do all at once. Just as with most things, go slowly. Implement changes over time so that you're able to fully integrate them into your life before you move on to the next thing. I know we always seem to be in a rush to lose weight—think of all the diets that have a finite time period as part of their name: the "21-Day Fix," *Whole30, The 4-Hour Body* (is that possible???)— but the truth is you've got all the time in the world to get this right. Take your time; go slow.

Who knows? You and I may end up turning into pretentious foodies and annoying all our friends!

Chapter Seven

· · · · · · ·

THE SOLUTION TO WILLPOWER, MODERATION, AND OTHER THINGS THAT DON'T WORK: THE TWO TABLES STRATEGY

E ach time I started a new diet (so basically every Monday morning) I would grit my teeth and summon my courage, as if steeling myself for a great battle. *This time will be different*, I would tell myself. *This time I will try harder, I won't cheat, I will follow all the diet's rules to the letter. This time I will have willpower!*

Well, that worked pretty well . . . until about 10:00 a.m., when I'd get hungry and the whole thing would land in the toilet. I'd stand over the kitchen sink, eating slice after slice of my beloved white-bread toast with butter and cinnamon sugar on it. (Much as I love bread, it's always been primarily a delivery system for fattening toppings as far as I'm concerned.) If I managed to last longer than a few hours, it was only by sheer force of will. As I said before, dieting always made me feel like I was holding my breath underwater. I could manage, but only for a short time—sooner or later I had to come up for air. When I'd inevitably give in to the cravings, I felt like I could finally breathe again.

For all those years I dieted and failed, I assumed what maybe you assume: that "diet experts" know what they're talking about with regard to willpower, "everything in moderation," and feelings of deprivation. We're told over and over again that we mustn't deny ourselves our favorite (read: unhealthy) foods, because if we do, we'll end up feeling deprived until we dive headfirst into a plate of nachos.

Bull cookies, I say.

WHY WILLPOWER IS A DISMAL WEIGHT-LOSS STRATEGY AND WHAT WORKS INSTEAD

If dieting left me feeling like I was holding my breath under-water, it's no wonder that I found it impossible to do it for very long. But this is what relying on willpower has always felt like to me: it takes so much mental energy to maintain that it is exhausting and unsustainable. When you cut yourself off from the one strategy you rely on to deal with stress—in my case, overeating—*and then put yourself in a very stressful situation* (dieting), it is doomed from the get-go.

But something very interesting happened to me when I decided to change my life. All of that gritting my teeth and steeling myself for the big fight fell away. In its place I learned discipline.

First, let's talk about the difference between willpower and discipline: as we saw in my failed attempts at dieting,

119

willpower is trying to white-knuckle it through a challenging situation by simply exerting your determination from out of thin air. For me it stirred up feelings of panic and fear. I felt as if I couldn't breathe, and there was a sense of futility to the whole thing, as if caving was somehow inevitable. There was a moral shortcoming implied in my failure. (*If only I would try harder*, I would berate myself.) Discipline, on the other hand, is a learned skill. Discipline comes from planning and preparation. Discipline is borne of a clear vision and specific goals. When you're disciplined you have direction; you understand your own limitations and compensate for those either by creating strategies that work for you or by drawing on the expertise of the specialized team you bring on board to support your efforts. Sound familiar?

"All right, that's great," you say. "But how does that help me when I walk into a meeting and there's a box of pillowy-soft, sugary magicalness (aka doughnuts) in the middle of the table?"

Are you ready for another visual? Come with me to my two tables. Picture this: There are two tables in front of you. One is modest sized and has lots of fruits and vegetables on it. There are lean proteins, some good-for-you convenience foods, healthy fats, whole grains, and a few treats. The foods on this table are all here because I consciously put them here. To be on this table, a given food must meet two important criteria, or it gets the boot.

1. It must be healthy.
2. I must absolutely *love* it—as in, can't-wait-to-eat-it-super-excited-every-time-it-shows-up-on-my-plate love.

That's it! It's very simple.

Now, the other table. That table is *huge*! It looks like a ginormous buffet table from my worst-nightmare restaurant. On that table is everything else: meats loaded with saturated fat, boatloads of processed foods, full-fat dairy, white bread and other grain products that have been stripped of nearly all of their nutritive value, sugary foods, and most restaurant food. See why it's such a big table?

Besides the fact that this is a very powerful visual tool for me—it clearly defines for me what I eat versus all possible food choices—it also illustrates an incredibly important principle that has guided my body transformation: I *choose* which table any given food goes on. I "place" it there myself. Intentionally.

As I began losing weight I started doing this as a self-protection tool. Remember, sometimes you must protect yourself from yourself! What I didn't learn until much later is that my trick has been proven to work for many who struggle to lose weight. In a 2012 study published in the *Journal of Consumer Research*, researchers split 120 students into two groups. One group was trained to use "I can't," while the other was trained to use "I don't." The results were stunning.

The students who told themselves "I can't eat *X*" chose to eat the chocolate candy bar 61 percent of the time. Meanwhile, the students who told themselves "I don't eat *X*" chose to eat the chocolate candy bar only 36 percent of the time. This simple change in terminology significantly improved the odds that each person would make a healthier food choice.

Fascinating. The reason this works so well, not just for me obviously, is that it's incredibly empowering to feel a sense of control over something that had felt very out of control all my life. Ben & Jerry's ice cream tormented me for years. I thought I should be able to control my desire for it. I just needed more willpower, right? And it's a bad idea to eliminate foods from your diet entirely, so we're told. (As I've said, this is baloney. More on "moderation" in a moment.) But consciously deciding which foods get to be on my table—which foods support my goals, which foods are good enough for me—is incredibly empowering. And even though Ben & Jerry's is definitely delicious, and I would indeed be very excited to see it on my plate, it doesn't meet the other criteria: it's not healthy. This one tool is incredibly liberating for me. No longer is it somehow a moral failure on my part that I cannot exert willpower over these foods. Instead, they simply do not make the cut because they don't meet the criteria to be on my table.

You may be surprised to learn that there are plenty of healthy foods that don't make the cut either; remember, the foods on my table aren't just there because they're healthy; I must *love* them too. I don't like green peppers, so they're not on my table. Likewise, I viscerally detest cantaloupe. Not on my table (you can have mine).

WHY I SAY "EVERYTHING IN MODERATION" IS CRAP

But why not just eat a moderate portion of unhealthy foods? Why banish them to that other table? After all, "everything in moderation!" is what we're told again and again by diet experts. As I said, their rationale is that banning the foods you love will set you up for disaster. If you eliminate your favorite foods from your diet, you will feel deprived. You'll end up craving them. You won't be able to resist the craving, and eventually you'll cave and then overeat them.

But hang on a second. This argument makes some assumptions that may make sense on an intellectual level, but not on an emotional or practical one. I know we all want weight loss to be a very left-brain, linear, logical process, but it isn't. Worse, this strategy just doesn't work—for me or for most dieters. It's a slippery slope that lands you right back in that hole you started in.

So what are the assumptions that the diet experts are making about the concept of "everything in moderation," and why do I think they're wrong?

1. They overestimate my honesty in determining a "moderate" portion. I kind of have my finger on the scale, if you know what I mean. I'm gonna fudge and call it good, "estimating" in my favor every time.

2. They underestimate my addiction. I'm no psychologist, and I don't pretend to be an expert on physiological addiction, but I can tell you a thing or two about my addictive behavior. Stuff gets stuck in my head, like an old LP record with a scratch; it just sits there and bumps over and over again until I can't stand it anymore, and I act on it. And by "acting on it," of course I mean stuffing all the cookies in my mouth.

IN EVERY SITUATION WHEN WE'RE CONFRONTED WITH A TEMPTATION THERE IS A MOMENT OF CHOICE.

3. They ignore the fact that most processed and restaurant foods were not created to be eaten in moderation. Remember those armies of chefs, food scientists, manufacturers, and marketers who work hard every day, doing their darndest to separate you from your money? Remember the evil, hyperpalatable foods that are nearly impossible to resist? I get that this is the game they want to play, but I don't have to play it.

So I don't.

I don't play their game, and I don't try to eat their food in moderation. Instead, I choose.

I choose how to spend my food dollars. I choose what goes in my grocery cart, what restaurants I patronize, and, ultimately, what goes in my mouth. I choose foods proactively. I place them on my table intentionally. All the crap food that doesn't meet my standard—remember, food on my table must be both healthy and outrageously delicious—is on that great big buffet table that I leave for someone who's a lot less picky than me.

Moderation doesn't work for me, and I'm gonna go out on a limb here and suggest that it doesn't work well for a lot of people. Just because it sounds reasonable doesn't mean it works. Again, I'm not interested in what diet experts say *should* work; I'm only interested in what actually *does* work.

But it's entirely possible that moderation works for you. Well, hallelujah and thank your lucky stars! That makes it a whole lot easier, for sure.

LEARNING TO CREATE SPACE BETWEEN CRAVING AND CAVING

I'm not going to stevia-coat this strategy for you; I was successful at developing my "two tables" strategy because my lap-band gave me a tool for creating space, if you will, between the moment of craving and the decision to give in to it. In this space I learned the difference between willpower and discipline. In every situation when we're confronted with a temptation there is a moment of choice. Sometimes it's no more than a nanosecond. Sometimes we're not even aware of it at all because we're caught off guard by an enticing smell (think about that cinnamon roll in the mall food court). But the moment does exist, even if only for a split second. After my surgery, when temptation crossed my path—in that split second of choice—I was reminded that the band itself limited the amount of food I could eat at any one time. (As I mentioned, it doesn't do that now because I don't have any fluid in the inner tube of my band, which means that, even though the band is still inside me, it no longer restricts how much I can eat.) In the early stages, the band's presence was a physical barrier and therefore a reminder of my commitment. Then—and even now—its presence underscores the commitment I made to my family and myself that this time around I resolved to change my habits forever.

In fact for me, the band took that nanosecond between craving and caving and opened it up like a wormhole; it became a passageway to self-awareness, self-acceptance, empowerment, and discipline. On a practical level, the band gave me the chance to think in that nanosecond that, *No, I don't really want that right now; in fact, that food doesn't really serve my goals at all. I think I'm just gonna set it on that other table.* Having self-awareness in that moment of choice was revolutionary for me. In opening up that space, I developed discipline and came up with strategies to help me deal with temptation—strategies such as the two tables.

Obviously, not everyone who reads this is going to have lap-band surgery, so how do you accomplish that "opening," that self-awareness, without the band? Believe me, if I knew, and if there were just one simple answer, I would share it with the world and end the obesity crisis! But I know the answer isn't starting a new diet every Monday morning, gritting your teeth and preparing to suffer through deprivation, relying on willpower. And I'm pretty sure it isn't trying to moderate the same trigger foods that I know would send me into an eating frenzy. I think that opening begins in the same place mine did, even before I had the surgery. I think it starts with a willingness to give up the idea that you must simply try harder.

You must try differently.

You must be willing to stop hiding behind the excuses, the rationalizations, and the justifications that keep you trapped. You must be willing to look objectively and ruthlessly at your own behavior, so you can create strategies that play to your strengths and manage your weaknesses. It's difficult. And it's scary, I know. But that's where self-awareness, self-acceptance, discipline, and, ultimately, empowerment are. And that's where success is too.

Chapter Eight

MY FOOD BLUEPRINT:
A FORMULA FOR EATING

You've been reading this book for a while now, and unless you skipped ahead to get to the "When's she gonna tell me what to eat on this diet?!?" part (and if you did, tsk, tsk, tsk, no cheating), you know me well enough to know that I'm not going to hand you a menu plan and fill the rest of the book's pages with recipes. (*Cough, cough. Easy way out!* Ahem.) Nowhere in this book will I tell you what you should eat. Never will I presume to know better than you do about what will work for you, for your family, and for your lifestyle.

Still, I recognize that it is useful to have an example of what a healthy eating plan looks like, so I lay mine out here. I call my style of eating a Food Blueprint because it's essentially a formula. Each meal and snack—five to six of them each day—has macronutrient elements (e.g., fat, protein, carbohydrates). And while it's always a good thing to expand our knowledge of nutrition, and I encourage you to do so, it's not necessary to hold a master's degree in nutrition science to lose weight. As long as you're filling your grocery cart with whole, unprocessed foods, cutting your sugar intake (seriously, it's more addictive than heroin), and *reducing your portion sizes*, you will lose weight and improve your health. How does it work? Giddyup, let's go.

A DAY ON MY PLATE

Stilettos are sexy.
Fast cars are sexy.
Some say facial hair is sexy (though generally only on men).

YOUR BODY WILL DO EXACTLY WHAT YOU TRAIN IT TO DO.

But let's be honest, schedules aren't sexy. Still, sticking to a schedule when it comes to your eating and exercise habits can make all the difference when it comes to weight-loss success. Schedules become routines, and routines become habits. Having healthy habits, behaviors that are seamlessly integrated into your life, is the key to long-term, permanent weight loss, because creating routines not only cements habits but also reinforces consistency. Whatever you do consistently is exactly the result you will get: If you exercise regularly, you will become fit. If you eat within your calorie range consistently, you will lose weight and then maintain that weight loss. Likewise, if your exercise and eating habits are haphazard and inconsistent, you will not achieve the results you want. Ultimately, your body will do exactly what you train it to do.

My eating plan is very consistent from day to day. I'm kind of a creature of habit anyway, but when you think about it, most of us tend to eat the same foods over and over again. As I said earlier, to be on my "table," those foods must meet two criteria: they must be healthy, and I must absolutely love them. It's enough variety for me, and as far as the things that I don't eat or drink anymore, the things that are on that other table? Well, I ate *a lot* of them—too much of them—for decades, so I kind of look at it as if I've already had my share of them. Even some of my old, familiar "diet foods" are on that other table. For years I had a powerful addiction to Diet Coke. Haven't touched the stuff in the years since I lost weight. Do I miss it? Nah, not really. I just sort of figure I've already had my lifetime supply, so I'm good.

I call my eating plan a Food Blueprint because it's not a specific meal plan so much as a formula for eating. I have very specific times of day that I eat and something I want to accomplish nutritionally with each meal or snack. It's important to me that I eat every two to four hours to manage my hunger. I find that when I get ravenously hungry, I tend to make poor food choices, grabbing the high-calorie, nutrient-poor treat rather than something that's aligned with my healthy-living goals. I have a Homer Simpson "D'oh!" moment every time I do it (still happens from time to time), but it's a good reminder that eating from my Food Blueprint is the best way of eating for me.

The Food Blueprint is a system of eating five to six mini-meals per day. Not revolutionary, to be sure, as lots of medical and weight-loss experts advocate for this approach. I find that it works for practical reasons, and I'm all about doing what actually works! There are four main reasons why this system works so well:

- Blood sugar stabilizes when you eat regularly, so you avoid high and low energy extremes throughout the day.
- Metabolism is fueled by two things: eating and exercising. You stoke the fire that keeps your metabolism burning when you eat.
- Hunger is kept in check so you don't become ravenously hungry (which triggers unplanned eating, usually of unhealthy foods).
- It's easier to practice discipline (this is *not* willpower, remember?) when you know you've got a yummy meal or snack coming soon!

So here's what a typical day on my plate looks like (see recipes section for many of my favorites):

6 a.m. Stumble out of bed, drink Metabolic Detox Tea—25 calories

8 a.m. Marilyn's First-Thing-in-the-Morning "Let's-Go-Get-It" Smoothie or Badass Green Protein Smoothie—400 calories

11 a.m. Post-workout snack: several options including my drop-dead, all-time-favorite Peanut Butter & Jelly Smoothie—300 calories

1 p.m. Lunch of Lentil Tomato Soup or Spicy Black-Bean Soup—250 calories

4 p.m. Afternoon snack: several options including my Vegan Thumbprint Cookie, almond milk, and an apple—350 calories

6:30 p.m. Dinner of one of my favorite salads, or veggies and lean protein—250 calories

9 p.m. Late-night snack of two Medjool dates or a small piece of dark chocolate—125 calories

You don't have to stick with my Food Blueprint. In fact, it's actually better if you figure out a system that works for you rather than trying to replicate mine. Mine adds up to approximately 1,700 calories a day, which is what I need to eat based on the weight I want to maintain and my activity level. The best part about the Food Blueprint is I can swap out the almond milk for a latte if I'm meeting someone at Starbucks, and I've been known to get pretty creative with a restaurant menu when I'm eating out, piecing together an off-menu entrée to meet my needs. If I'm traveling or just having a really busy day, I'll do the best I can with what's available to me and what I've got stashed in a small cooler or my purse. I'm not big on spontaneous eating, but when I haven't planned ahead, I always choose to fill up on vegetables and lean protein first, then healthy fats, then fruit, and then whole grains after that, if I'm still hungry.

CHEESE IS CRACK.

So maybe schedules aren't sexy, but for me, keeping a consistent routine means that I don't battle with myself about whether or not I feel like going to the gym or eating healthy. And frankly, I don't try to squeeze healthy living behaviors into my busy life. I have healthy living behaviors that I build my life around.

A FEW FOOD RULES TO LIVE BY

All the previously mentioned strategies, principles, and visualizations are great, but I also have a list of down-'n'-dirty food rules that guide what I eat, when I eat, and how I eat. Though none will probably shock you, taken together and combined with the strategies that make up most of this chapter, these rules help me proactively structure my eating habits.

I've said it before: all diets have rules. Whether we're told to count points or eat like a caveman (er, cavewoman) or eat their prepackaged food, every diet has a set of rules that we're supposed to adhere to. We're told that if we follow the diet's rules, we'll lose weight. Well, that may be true, but how often have you gotten tired of the rules and ended up bending them so often that they weren't really hard-and-fast rules anymore so much as "suggestions"? Yeah, me too.

When I committed to changing my habits forever, I decided to make my own rules. Following other people's rules never worked very well for me, but as I began listening to myself, setting goals, and constructing a new life, I realized something really important: I have much higher standards than I had ever given myself credit for. Way back at the outset of my journey, when I had the pivotal thought that I was worth the time and energy to do what I needed to do to get better, I set out creating an entirely new set of rules.

So now these are the food rules that I live by—along with the guiding principles and far-reaching strategies that I outlined before:

1. I don't eat spontaneously.
2. My eating plan lacks only one thing: variety (that is, I tend to eat the same healthy foods over and over again).
3. I eat off salad plates.
4. Cheese is crack. Sugar too. Limit these as much as possible.
5. It's okay to have a Butterfinger bar (or three) for dinner on Halloween night.

6. I don't get all caught up in nutritional hype and scientific mumbo jumbo. (Makes my head hurt and has little to do with weight loss. Remember, weight loss isn't an intellectual problem.)

7. I spend time on Sundays planning and shopping for the week's meals.

8. I am not a cow; I do not graze. (See above ban on spontaneous eating.)

9. I don't drink alcohol. (Mostly. Ahem. A girl likes a beer on a hot, sunny day sometimes.)

10. Most of my foods don't have labels. (That is, they look like they did when they came from the ground.)

11. I am not a garbage disposal. (I spent years finishing off the scraps of half-eaten PBJs that had been discarded by a two-year-old. Nope. Done.)

12. I read labels and don't eat ingredients that I can't pronounce.

13. I eat moderate, reasonable portions, and I don't patronize establishments that serve gargantuan, obscene portions.

14. I don't eat in my car, nor do I eat anything that could potentially be served from a drive-thru window. (There is a Starbucks venti-decaf-americano exclusion to this rule, it should be noted.)

15. I don't eat directly out of the package or from a serving container, because I lose track of the portion size. (See the "cheese is crack" rule, which stems directly from my fondness for eating shredded cheese right out of the bag as my dog sits under me, waiting for me to drop some.)

16. I don't eat bread and dessert in the same meal. (As far as our bodies are concerned, they're the same thing.)

17. I don't eat dessert after lunch. (When did this become a thing?)

18. After I've eaten my portion of food, I brush my teeth or pop a piece of gum or a breath mint in my mouth. For me, getting the taste of food out of my mouth and having that clean, minty-fresh taste instead means I won't go back for seconds.

19. I don't eat within three hours of bedtime. Other than a bite of chocolate or a couple of sweet dates, any kind of heavy food close to bedtime sits like lead in my stomach and makes it hard for me to sleep.

Having said all of this, never, ever, *ever* substitute anyone else's judgment for your own. Nobody knows you better than you, and as long as you're willing to be honest with yourself (and check in with your doctor, of course), nobody can figure out rules that will work better for you than *you*!

The reason these rules work so well for me is that I took the time to understand my behavior and create new habits based on my lifestyle and my values. These rules are as individualized to me as my fingerprints, but you're welcome to try them out and see if they work for you.

Food should be pleasurable, no doubt. Where we get into trouble is when eating becomes one of our *only* sources of pleasure. When that happens, it crosses an invisible line from pleasure into hedonistic eating, wreaking havoc on our self-esteem and our health.

GET MOVING!
HOW EXERCISE HELPED ME HEAL

Though we tend to overemphasize the importance of exercise in weight loss—*The Biggest Loser* aside, most of the important stuff happens in the kitchen—exercise helped me lose another twenty-five pounds two years after my initial eighty-five-pound weight loss after lap-band surgery. Maybe even more important, exercise has helped me rehabilitate my wounded relationship with my body.

I found that when I exercised I wasn't self-conscious. I felt powerful and capable. I learned to make my exercise time sacrosanct and came to appreciate having that time to dedicate to my own health and well-being. I've been a worrier all my life, but through exercise I found a way to release my anxiety that before I'd always tried to numb with food. As if stress relief and a sense of empowerment weren't reason enough to exercise, my cardiovascular health has vastly improved, I sleep better, and, well, it's just plain fun!

Early on in my journey I started taking long walks. After years of having no privacy (with little ones practically Velcroed to my legs), I loved being outdoors, alone. I could go at my own pace, listen to music I wanted to listen to (no *Dora the Explorer* sound track anywhere to be found), and go for as long as it suited me. At first it was just a mile or two, but before long it was seven or eight miles. Those walks became more focused as I strove to go farther and faster. At some point my fast walk just morphed into a run, and that unlikely beginning is how I became a runner. The first few months were arduous; at times I would remind myself that no, I was indeed *not* going backward! It felt so slow and difficult. In the beginning, in fact, I only ran on the downhills, walking uphill and on the flat. But I kept at it, and before long I was running on the straightaways too. I got faster and gained confidence. Building strength in my legs and getting my breathing under control meant I gained the stamina to run uphill, and within six months of starting to run I ran my first 10K (6.2 miles) race. I pushed myself, running four days a week, farther and faster. In another three months I ran my first half marathon. One year to the date after that, I ran my first marathon (26.2 miles). To say that I am proud of that accomplishment would be an understatement. For this former fat girl, my triumph felt complete when I crossed that finish line. This victory felt wholly my own; I knew how hard I had worked to lose weight, to work through my emotional eating, to become an athlete, and to run a marathon at age forty-eight. I wore the medal around for a week. I fully intend to have my finishing time (4:35, still my personal best) put on my tombstone. I was positively giddy.

Unfortunately, running led to injuries, as it does for most people. Happily, the first of those serious injuries led me to yoga. Subsequent running injuries led me to swimming and cycling. I also took up strength training and tried my hand at ballroom dancing, skydiving, zip-lining, and rock climbing. Belly dancing, anyone? Honestly, I've found that moving my body, getting outside of my comfort zone, is so rewarding. I've made more new friends than I can count pursuing all of my new activities, but I've also brought along lots of dear friends for the ride.

NOW, EVERY MORNING WHEN MY FEET HIT THE FLOOR, I RECOMMIT TO THE HABITS THAT I KNOW WILL KEEP ME FIT AND HEALTHY, AND EVERY DAY THAT I WORK TOWARD THAT COMMITMENT I FEEL SO BLESSED.

For me, exercise has brought a sense of accomplishment, become my number-one stress reliever, and taught me that even a middle-aged mom can cut loose, have fun, and be a total badass. I've come to realize that I'm a lot tougher than I gave myself credit for, back when I was obese. My tough workouts taught me that making good food choices seems pretty damn easy compared to some of the extremely difficult physical challenges that I've put myself up against; and I've finally discovered what it feels like to be comfortable in my own skin.

THE PHYSICALITY PRINCIPLE

Maybe nobody appreciates being fit more than somebody who used to be morbidly obese. Now, every morning when my feet hit the floor, I recommit to the habits that I know will keep me fit and healthy, and every day that I work toward that commitment I feel so blessed. Physical fitness feels like an incredible gift, and I view the time that I spend investing in my health each day as a privilege.

Having spent most of my life feeling detached from my physical body because of my weight, I know all too well what it feels like to inhabit a body that brings nothing but shame. As I was losing weight, though, I began to feel better, physically and emotionally. On those long walks I mentioned, I enjoyed the sensation of my muscles as they were working. I felt vital and alive. I even came to appreciate the next-day soreness I often experienced. Those achy muscles meant that I was getting stronger. I gained awareness of my physical body, and I came to feel a sense of ownership of it and responsibility toward it.

Maybe it's all the yoga I do now, but I really believe in a mind-body connection. That is, I believe that our human experience is physical, emotional, and spiritual. If you're detached from one—as I was detached from my physical body for so long—then you are detached from the others. Becoming connected to my physical body through exercise brought me in touch with my spiritual and emotional self. Tapping into those parts of who I authentically am is the very core of self-acceptance, and I know in my heart of hearts that I could not have achieved permanent weight loss if I had not found self-acceptance. Mindfulness—self-awareness—is how you overcome the habits and behaviors of emotional eating, but self-acceptance is the antidote for it.

Though I viscerally felt the healing power of exercise ever since I laced up my shoes for those walks early on, it wasn't until an outing with a couple of girlfriends a while back that I could articulate its importance in my overall success. On that day, my friends and I had gone to a barre class together and afterward were enjoying an espresso and one another's companionship as a rich reward after a tough workout. We were sitting in a little French bakery that had all manner of tempting treats in the glass display case: brioche, croissants, and my personal favorite, *pain au chocolat*. Oh, man, they looked good! While we were sitting there drinking our coffee, we found ourselves engrossed in conversation about how the exercise we do, while really good for us and helpful in maintaining our weight and health, is primarily beneficial because it puts us in touch with our physical bodies.

We all agreed that the more in touch we are with our physical bodies, the less likely we are to abuse them (i.e., to eat *pain au chocolat* on a regular basis). And by *abuse*, we weren't just talking about overeating. Certainly there are other hugely damaging behaviors that some of us inflict on our bodies (drug and alcohol addictions, cigarette smoking), but goodness knows there are so many smaller abuses to which we subject ourselves. We all admitted to occasionally shortchanging our sleep in favor of staying up and watching late-night TV, and then walking around like zombies the next day, too tired to exercise or make good food choices. I was so guilty of this when my kids were little; I always felt like I got a second wind after I got them off to bed. And, my girlfriends and I agreed, there were the less obvious abuses we inflict on ourselves, like failing to see a doctor regularly for checkups and preventative care. Or maybe we take on the burden of other people's problems and then let resentment and anger smolder inside. These kinds of neglect and stress—whether they're self-inflicted (not getting enough sleep), forced upon us (other people's "issues"), or simply the result of passive procrastination fueled by denial (neglecting to schedule a mammogram)—are all ways of abusing our bodies and undermining our healthy habits and good intentions.

It was really my own experience breaking through the inertia of my sedentary lifestyle, pushing outside my comfort zone to try new workouts, and eventually coming to define myself as an athlete that helped me name what I call the "Physicality Principle." As my girlfriends and I agreed in that coffee shop, feeling connected to our physical bodies gives us an appreciation for our bodies' innate strength and beauty and also a sense of responsibility to care for them.

There's something so primal about the link between our physical, emotional, and spiritual selves: when we respect and love our physical bodies, we treat them with care. We give them the best possible fuel. We work them to their limits because we know that in so doing we become stronger and more resilient. We come to realize that our bodies are amazing tools and awesome gifts. We bear a responsibility to take good care of the one we're given.

Being in touch with my physical body, through self-care and healthy habits, means so much to me now. Not only will I spend more years in a strong body, but I will also just feel good, from head to toe. And what I know for sure is that this feeling doesn't have anything to do with what the outside world deems "beautiful." Instead it comes from being physically, emotionally, and spiritually at peace. All the sweat equity that I invest each day is paid back to me tenfold in improved health and mended self-esteem.

THE VICIOUS CYCLE VS. THE VIRTUOUS CYCLE

Because of the Physicality Principle, exercise becomes the key to unlocking successful weight loss. Why? Because it breaks the power of what I call the "vicious cycle." You know the one:

Overeat → feel physically sick → skip workout → feel guilty → repeat.

I was imprisoned in the vicious cycle for more than twenty years. I know how helpless it feels. The vicious cycle held me in its powerful grip all those years for two reasons:

THE TIME I SPEND EXERCISING, THE EFFORT I MAKE PREPARING HEALTHY MEALS, AND THE ENERGY I PUT INTO PRIORITIZING WELLNESS IN MY LIFE IS SACRED. IT IS INVIOLATE. IT IS NONNEGOTIABLE.

1. It's a habit. More accurately, it's a whole buncha habits combined. When I finally broke through, it was because I forced myself to become conscious of my bad habits instead of operating on autopilot. The power of that decision gave me the courage to start building good habits, one by one.

141

2. It's steeped in complex emotions. Seriously, I needed
    hip waders for this stuff. I was in deep denial that
    my behavior was self-destructive. I was the queen of
    excuses: *I'm just stressed out today because of the kids.
    I don't have time to prepare healthy food. I deserve this
    treat because I work so hard and give so much to so
    many.* Also, I was paralyzed with fear that I wouldn't
    be able to cope without relying on food. I felt over-
    whelmed by hopelessness that I'd ever be able to make
    a dent in my problem. And I was filled with shame that
    I was unable to control myself and stick to a plan.

So how do you even begin to break free of the cycle's
hold? Again, my lap-band was an advantage early on. When
the inner tube of the band is filled with saline, the opening is
constricted, limiting the amount of food I could eat in any one
sitting. I physically couldn't eat large portions—not quickly,
anyway. Part of the "disease" of obesity, if you'll grant a lay-
person permission to deem it such, is the mindlessness and,
frankly, the speed with which we eat. The band's restriction
made that frenzied eating impossible. Oh, I could still eat the
same amount of food *eventually*, it would just have taken me a
lot longer to do it, and over time I got tired of my meals taking
so long. It was easier to simply reduce my portion sizes and eat
more frequently (the five to six mini-meals per day I outlined
in the Food Blueprint).

Because I was no longer able to mindlessly eat hundreds,
if not thousands, of extra calories, the lap-band helped throw
a wrench into my vicious cycle. Remember, this is the pattern:

Overeat → feel physically sick → skip workout → feel guilty → repeat.

Since it was nearly impossible for me to overeat, I no longer felt physically sick from doing so. Because I no longer felt

physically sick from overeating, I felt better, and eventually I started taking those long walks I mentioned earlier. These small changes began to come together in a pattern of positive, self-reinforcing good habits that became the virtuous cycle:

Make good food choices → feel better → choose to exercise →
feel empowered → repeat.

The virtuous cycle isn't virtuous in the sense that it's some sort of moral high ground; it's virtuous simply because these are principled behaviors that are aligned with our healthy living goals. When our actions are aligned with our goals we sleep better at night, and we expend a whole lot less energy beating ourselves up over our "failings."

Breaking the vicious cycle is very difficult. Nobody appreciates this more than somebody who was morbidly obese for twenty-plus years. My lap-band helped me interrupt the cycle at the overeating stage, but certainly not everybody who's trapped in the vicious cycle is going to have weight-loss surgery, nor do they need to. Fortunately, it's possible to break the cycle anywhere along the sequence.

Daily (or very-near-daily) exercise also breaks the vicious cycle. I could easily have relapsed, just like the 60 percent or more of people who have weight-loss surgery do. Patients get sneaky about "outsmarting" their surgical restrictions by eating high-calorie foods that go down easily. It's part of the disease of obesity to be steeped in denial about our self-destructive ways. But I didn't go that route. I owe my long-term success to the connection I made with my physical body—a connection that I can only achieve through exercise. Staying in the virtuous cycle—consistently making the right food choices, exercising, feeling connected to our physical bodies, and feeling empowered by our choices—is how we lose weight and keep it off for the rest of our lives.

Is it hard? Pfffft, don't be ridiculous. Of course it's hard! When have you ever done anything worth doing that wasn't hard? But I swear it gets easier, and we're so damn worth it.

I SCHEDULE MY EXERCISE TIME AS IF I WERE MEETING WITH THE PRESIDENT OR THE POPE; IN OTHER WORDS, THE TIME IS SACROSANCT

I love that word: *sacrosanct*. I'm gonna start throwing it around in dinner party conversation. Does it make me sound smart? Hmmmm, maybe not. The reason it's relevant in this context is that it speaks to so many issues related to health, wellness, and fitness. The time I spend exercising, the effort I make preparing healthy meals, and the energy I put into prioritizing wellness in my life is sacred. It is inviolate. It is nonnegotiable.

Now, I've never met a president or a pope, but I gather that you don't *try* to make time for them; you don't *hope* to get there on time. They're important people, and you would make that appointment a priority above all else. Likewise, my exercise time is important too. In terms of my lifelong health, it's much more important than meeting someone famous. So frequently I hear people say, "I'm gonna try to get to the gym this week," or "I hope I don't gain weight on vacation." We can *try* and *hope* ourselves till the cows come home, but that's not going to get us anywhere. Just like willpower is a poor weight-loss strategy, pinning our commitment to exercise on good intentions isn't gonna cut it. People tell me all the time, "I just don't feel motivated to work out!" as if they're waiting for a wave of motivation to come crashing over them, transforming them into somebody who springs out of bed each morning and can't wait to work out. Well, maybe that's true for some people, but what I found is that I'm much better off treating exercise like all my other healthy-living habits. I plan, prepare, and commit my way to success. That's discipline.

In terms of my exercise regimen, this means identifying time by first recognizing and eliminating those time wasters that we talked about, and then by refusing to let other things crowd this new space. I like to say, "I don't make excuses not to work out; I make excuses why I can't do other stuff because

NOW I KNOW THAT BY KEEPING MY PROMISES TO MYSELF, I HONOR MYSELF AND MY LOVED ONES BY CARING FOR THE GREATEST GIFT I HAVE BEEN GIVEN, MY BODY.

I gotta go work out." (Every time I say that it makes me laugh, partly because it sounds so badass, but partly because it stands in opposition to the way most people operate.)

To achieve this I had to bulletproof my workout time. Oh, I'll reschedule stuff if I have to, cancel things, and throw the word *No!* around plenty so that I don't miss a workout. Why? For all the reasons we've talked about before, but primarily because consistency is the key to fitness. Now that exercise is a regular part of my everyday life, there's a certain rhythm to it, and I miss it when it's not there. Being consistent in my exercise regimen is the only way to ensure that my body gets all the benefits of cardiovascular conditioning and strength training. And consistency also gives me that daily reminder of how good my body feels when I work it, what my muscles feel like while they're working and when they're at rest. That sensation, that physical cue, is my way of staying in tune with my body, and it reinforces my commitment to do good things for it. That's the power of the Physicality Principle and the virtuous cycle working together!

Goal setting is another part of that equation. I'm usually training for something, which means that my workouts are planned out and progressive. Each one builds on the last, and the effect is cumulative. The point of a workout is not simply to burn calories; the point is to get stronger, get faster, go longer, get better! Each workout has a purpose, so I don't want to miss a single one.

But maybe the single most important reason I make time to exercise every day is just because it's fun! Okay, not fun the same way that going shopping is fun or watching the big game is fun, but yes, it's fun. I'm sending another paradigm shift your way, so get ready to catch it.

Visualize an idyllic scene of children playing happily, laughing, and smiling. Are they at a park playing on the swings, or are they building a snowman and dressing him up with rock eyes and a carrot nose? Whatever you pictured doesn't need to have been part of your own childhood; it could be a scene from a movie or just an imagined scene, but the point is that the children are blissfully absorbed in what they're doing, without concern for the passing of time or their next task. They are completely engaged and having a blast!

How often as adults do we give ourselves permission to do the same thing? What would that type of activity look like for you? Can you remember a time when you were so completely focused on something that you lost track of time, and hours had passed in a span of what seemed like minutes? It could be with others; it could be alone. You may not yet know what this activity will be, and that's okay. Also, it may not be a happy-go-lucky kind of activity; for me it's running. I'm not skipping along humming a happy tune and picking wildflowers while running. No, I'm focused like a laser with every cell in my body fully present and absorbed in the task at hand. I can lose myself and my sense of time (well, I do wear a watch that gives me time/distance/pace, but that's all part of the fun). But what I mean is that there is nothing in the universe as compelling at that moment as what I am doing. It's completely exhilarating and deeply satisfying.

Each of us needs to have these active pursuits that bring us this kind of pleasure. (Lose yourself in your knitting if you want to, but you *know* that's not what I'm talking about.) When you discover what that physical endeavor is for you and then do it consistently, you will not only stick with your exercise plan, you will look forward to doing it.

The time that I make for exercise is sacrosanct, but so is the commitment itself. It was difficult at first. Though I felt resolved to change, I faced both internal and external challenges to that resolve; I will discuss some of those in the next chapter. But despite the challenges, I found that when I made exercise a priority in my life, I made *my life* a priority in my life. And now I know that by keeping my promises to myself, I honor myself and my loved ones by caring for the greatest gift I have been given: my body.

CROSS-TRAINING AND COMFORT ZONES

Cross-training is the term used to describe the combining of different forms of exercise that complement each other. The effectiveness of one compensates for the limitations of the other. We've got to work muscles from different directions to maximize results. Just like anything else, if we do the same thing over and over again we see diminishing returns on our effort.

We also want to keep our routine from getting stale. If I'm not looking forward to a workout, then I know it's time to change things up. I want each one to be fun but challenging, and maybe even a little bit of a stretch. I do different activities on different days of the week; I'll mix up a group class or two with some solo activities. In the warmer months I'll even ride my bike to get to my exercise class! Variety is the spice of life, and where exercise is concerned it also prevents boredom and burnout—two surefire ways to throw your exercise routine on the skids.

Cross-training doesn't just sound cool, it is cool. More important, it's absolutely vital to our long-term success. It's so easy to overwork the big muscles that are already pretty strong; our quadriceps and gluteus muscles are powerful and tend to dominate weaker muscles like the hamstrings. But ask any runner and they'll tell you: you ignore your hamstrings at your peril. When the hamstrings aren't strong enough relative to quadriceps, they can get pulled or strained. This imbalance increases the possibility of a knee injury such as an ACL (anterior cruciate ligament) tear. Women tend to have more problems with this type of injury than men do because of the angle of our hips relative to our knees, and our tendency to let the quadriceps dominate. This is true of the hip stabilizer muscles as well. The hip flexors, abductors, and external rotators all

THERE'S NO GROWTH INSIDE OUR COMFORT ZONES—JUST NONE.

support the hip joint, but when they're too weak to support the work we want them to do, it places undue stress on the knee and the iliotibial (IT) band (a thick strip of connective tissue that joins several muscles in the lateral thigh).

While it's interesting to know all of that, it's more important to simply approach fitness in a balanced way so that we don't overtax any one set of muscles. The best way to accomplish that is by doing lots of different kinds of workouts. And truthfully, the more forms of exercise we try, the greater the chance that we'll find things we absolutely love. Because if we don't enjoy it, exercise will seem like a burden, just one more thing on our never-ending to-do list. And that is a recipe for disaster.

But trying new things can be intimidating, right? The thought of exercising in any kind of public setting (a gym, a class, outdoors, or—*gasp!*—a pool) can be terrifying, especially if you're overweight or obese. I get that, but two thoughts:

1. Nobody's paying any attention to you, because they're too caught up in thinking about themselves, and
2. If they are judging you, well, that says a whole lot more about them than it does about you, doesn't it?

I'm a creature of habit, and I'd run every day if I could, but having several injuries and then knee surgery has meant that I've had to branch out and try new things. I was dragged— kicking and screaming, I might add—to hot yoga more than four years ago. It would be a good workout while I healed from a stress fracture, a friend told me. Because it's done in a room that is kept at 105 degrees and 40 percent humidity, and it takes some getting used to, that's for sure. But, as I said, the heat, the deep stretching, and the peaceful meditative quality of it make my little heart sing. I have come to love this practice and now do it several times a week. My body craves it, and I never would've known that if I hadn't been willing to give it a try.

Just before my knee surgery a couple of years ago, my orthopedic surgeon and I were discussing my healing and rehabilitation. We discussed exercise: because I wouldn't be able to put any weight on my leg for six weeks, I literally had no other option than swimming. Now, I was not a swimmer. In fact, largely because of the shame I felt about my body and the prospect of wearing a bathing suit in public, I hadn't been swimming since I took lessons at the YMCA when I was nine years old. I didn't understand the breathing, and what about my contacts?!? Am I supposed to take 'em out? I'm blind as a bat! But I decided that the greater goal of maintaining my fitness was more important than my discomfort at trying something new, so I signed up for adult group swimming lessons. The instructor taught us some basic skills, and it gave me the confidence to start swimming on my own. After a couple of months I could swim more than a mile in the pool. I dropped weight, sculpted my upper body, and, even better, discovered that I absolutely love swimming!

My point is, there's no growth inside our comfort zones— just none. We must keep pushing into new territory to keep our workouts interesting, to tax muscles in different ways, and to find new things that get us jacked up. There is a whole world of fun workouts out there, but we're gonna miss out on it if we're not willing to reach outside our comfort zones.

Even though forging into the great unknown is daunting, nobody said you have to do it alone! Enlist a friend, drag one of your kids, invite your mom. I've been known to post on

Facebook that I'm gonna go try a new workout and would anybody like to join me? Why not?!? I find it's so much easier to
face a new workout when I'm with another brave soul and we
can compare notes afterward. And in that case, there's nearly
always a tall skinny latte involved after we've pushed outside
our comfort zones too.

YOU MUST INTRINSICALLY ENJOY IT OR IT WON'T LAST

Does everybody have an inner athlete? I dunno. I do know that
120 pounds ago I would've told you that *I* didn't have one.
   Turns out, I was wrong.
   I do have an inner athlete, and I have harnessed her
strength and drive to finally put to rest the food demons that
tormented me most of my life.
   Becoming an athlete means that I have learned to trust
my body and myself. I know that I am made of some seriously
tough stuff, because I prove that over and over again—with
every race, every challenging workout, and every time I decide
not to stay up late or go out and drink too much because I've
got an important workout in the morning.
   Exercise has so many lessons to teach about finding passion,
discipline, and drive, each of which is essential to transformational change. Among the most important of those lessons is
that if you don't intrinsically enjoy what you're doing, it won't
last. When I applied that principle to food, I came up with my
strategy of the two tables. Remember, a food must be healthy
to be on my table, but I must absolutely love it too. If I didn't
love all of the healthy foods on my table, I would end up feeling
deprived or get frustrated. I wouldn't be able to maintain my
new eating habits. This same principle works in fitness too. So

while exercise is important for the myriad health benefits and the calories we burn, it should also be a kickass good time!

If that hasn't been your experience before, then you're in for quite a treat. The way you tap into the fun is by figuring out what floats your boat. That is, what kind(s) of exercise do you find pleasurable? Don't worry if you don't know the answer to that question right now. Remember, though, we're not talking about "fun" in the same way that going shoe shopping (ahem, I have a slight shoe problem) or getting pedis with your gal pals is fun. I mean "fun" as in challenging, stimulating, exciting, exhilarating. The kind where you feel a sense of accomplishment at the end. The kind where you feel a bit of bravado afterward because you just did something pretty damn amazing.

Yeah, that kind of fun.

That kind of fun is addictive (maybe even more so than a new pair of shoes). Simply put, it is a rush.

That rush transforms exercise from something you "should" do into something you can't wait to do!

Here's how it works for me: I get bored really easily; I mentioned I have the attention span of a gnat. My workouts need to be mentally challenging, not just physically challenging. For that reason, I like swimming and yoga: both require my full attention, as I need to be very aware of my body position and good form. I also enjoy moving toward a goal, so training for specific events meets this need for me. Whether it's a running race or a triathlon, I like the buildup and structure of a specialized regimen.

I've also figured out that I like some solo workouts and some social ones. I love the communal energy of a spinning class, but I always run alone. Maybe you enjoy the camaraderie and accountability of a softball team or meeting a friend after work for a group Zumba class. Whichever kind of exerciser you are—and if you're like me, you may be a little bit of both—take the time to discover what you really, truly love. Whether it's the competitiveness of racing or the solitude of being out on the water, sculling at dawn, go on a search for the workouts that feed your soul. Ultimately, it's less important what we do than why we do it.

When I dug in to find my inner athlete, she didn't emerge right away. I searched. I stumbled. I pulled over and asked for directions. But in my searching, I found her. Along the way, I came to realize that I wasn't just building sweat equity toward physical fitness; I was creating a life that was full of new purpose and meaning. So now *athlete* is a moniker I wear just as proudly as I wear *wife, mother,* and *writer.* I'm betting you'll wear it well too.

A FEW EXERCISE RULES TO LIVE BY

I've always resented rules, but that's because they were somebody else's rules. I found success with creating an eating plan that worked for me when I wrote my own rule book. Similarly, the exercise rules I live by are uniquely mine. (Though admittedly, I think they're pretty universally true.)

1. I make rigorous exercise a part of every day. (Or very nearly so.)
2. I can't exercise and be self-conscious at the same time; it stifles my workout.
3. While doing cardio, I listen to music that I cannot possibly sit still for. (Please note, I have moves like Jagger.)
4. When I get injured, I immediately see my doctor and/ or sports medicine doctor to help me figure out what's wrong and get back on track. In the meantime, I find other forms of exercise that help me stay true to the bigger goal: lifelong fitness.

5. I refer to myself as an athlete. I make friends with and support other athletes.

6. I invest in exercise equipment and clothing that is the best I can afford and appropriate for my level of experience and use.

7. I follow and attend sporting events for female athletes.

8. I use a trainer to help me reach my fitness goals.

9. I look for opportunities to be active, no matter what I'm doing. (Like taking the stairs, parking farther away, and so on. All that little stuff that we think doesn't matter? Yeah, it matters.)

10. I encourage others to be active with me.

I'm no spring chicken, that's for sure. Each passing year I feel like having a little ceremony for the latest body part that creaks and aches. But I ran my first marathon at age forty-eight. My septuagenarian mother (translation: she's in her seventies) and I run a 12K race together in our hometown of Spokane, Washington, every spring. Physical fitness isn't just for twentysomethings. In fact, go ahead and quote me when I say that I've found the fountain of youth. And guess what? It's our own damn sweat!

Chapter Ten

THE PRICE OF CHANGE:
WHAT PRICE WILL YOU PAY?

How could there be a downside to eating healthier? Or to exercising more? How could it be a bad thing to put yourself first? How could there possibly be negative consequences to losing weight??? Ha! There's always a price to pay.

We've already touched on some of the difficulties that can pop up along the way—the saboteurs, our own internal conflicts—but it cannot be overemphasized: there is a price to pay for changing your lifestyle and losing weight. Think about it: if there were only an upside, nobody would be overweight!

This is the hardest part. This is the reason diets fail. This is the part that nobody talks about. You can count calories or points from now until the end of time, but if you don't account for the fact that changing your lifestyle will have consequences—and then prepare to face those consequences head-on—you will fail.

The truth is, everyone who successfully loses weight and keeps it off pays a cost. You will too. I wish I could tell you exactly what that cost will be, but I can't because it's different for everybody. Mine was mercifully low. Yours could be high. The higher the cost, the more difficult the journey to wellness will be. I'm sorry; I don't mean to scare you. I just want you to be prepared.

In no particular order, here are some of the often-overlooked consequences of changing your lifestyle and losing weight:

1. It's expensive.
2. It's time consuming.
3. It changes the nature of some relationships.
4. You no longer get to hide behind denial, fear, martyrdom, self-doubt, or whatever other neuroses have held you back.

Take a deep breath. Here we go.

IT'S EXPENSIVE

My first attempt at dieting came at age ten when my mother dropped me off at a Weight Watchers meeting. I used to joke that I was a lifetime member, not because I ever reached my goal weight, but because I often felt as if I'd been doing it my entire lifetime. Though my journey was long, I never made any effort to calculate how much money I spent on all my various go-arounds at weight loss.

If I attempted to add it all up, I'd have to include hundreds of Weight Watchers meetings (in addition to that first meeting, I started and quit dozens of times), my bookshelves overflowing with diet books and cookbooks, my stash of audiotapes and CDs that promised to either motivate or hypnotize me thin, and all the pre-packaged-food diet plans I signed on for where I bought their food, plus the others where it was delivered to my front door. Through the years I also purchased gym memberships, exercise classes, and fitness equipment, including weights, "ab rollers," resistance bands, and workout DVDs that promised me a Brazilian butt (spoiler alert: I still don't have one). Oh, and how could I forget all of the medical professionals I saw, including doctors, nutritionists, and therapists?

THE REALITY IS THAT MOST OF US NEED HELP LOSING WEIGHT, AND THAT HELP SOMETIMES COSTS MONEY.

Given that I did all of that for decades—almost constantly—the total is probably pretty close to the $18,000 I spent on my lap-band procedure. As I said before, some insurance companies cover the cost of bariatric surgery for some patients; mine didn't. We paid for the surgery by refinancing our house. It was a significant sacrifice for my family, and I have a lot of respect for that sacrifice. I would not have spent the money if I hadn't been absolutely certain that I was ready to make all the permanent lifestyle changes that were necessary for the surgery to be successful.

Whether weight-loss surgery is in your future or not, there are financial costs involved in living a healthy lifestyle. I think it's fair to point out, though, that there are also *huge* costs to not losing weight: higher health-care costs, having to buy and take medications for conditions related to obesity, lost workdays due to those conditions, reduced functionality and mobility, depression and misery, and the granddaddy of them all, a shorter lifespan. You could make an argument that you're going to pay one way or another, and it's just a matter of *when* and *how*. If you maintain the status quo, not all of the money is going to come out of your checkbook in one lump sum, but the costs are there just the same. Of course, you can't put a dollar value on some of the downsides of being fat (how much does it cost to be miserable?), and we both know that you and every-one around you "pays" when you're suffering.

For me to make healthy eating and exercise a top prior-ity, I had to reorganize our family budget. I think it's only fair that we take an honest look at the costs of a healthy lifestyle upfront. It's certainly not required or anything, but I like to have lots of fitness options; that means that I own lots of exer-cise equipment. When I bought my bike a couple of years ago, it was more valuable than my car (which really isn't saying much considering I was driving a thirteen-year-old minivan at the time, but you get the point: bikes can be pricey). Over the years, my husband (a fitness buff himself) and I have built an impressive home gym that includes a treadmill, an elliptical machine, a weight bench, lots of dumbbells, and a variety of other pieces of equipment. (If you see me in the grocery store, please ask me about my BOSU ball and why I love it so much.)

Other expenses related to losing weight may include a gym membership, exercise classes at a studio (seriously, tell me you'll try yoga), hiring a personal trainer, seeing a nutri-tionist, going to a therapist, buying new clothes as you change sizes, and shopping for healthier food. The costs of these items vary wildly. Exercise equipment is often expensive new, but can be purchased slightly used (try Craigslist or a secondhand sporting goods store like Play It Again Sports if you have one in your area). Choose activities that have a low cost of entry (i.e., *not* cycling). A good pair of running/walking shoes costs about one hundred dollars, and you're good to go! Replacing your entire wardrobe is costly, but needn't be done all at once, and who doesn't love shopping for new clothes? There are worse problems to have than needing to buy smaller pants!

Shopping for healthier food can be an adjustment. I am truly a path-of-least-resistance shopper, so I haven't changed *where* I shop so much as what goes in my cart. I spend a lot more time in the produce section now than I do buying Hamburger Helper or Lunchables. (Okay, I never buy those anymore.) The great news is that even my neighborhood Safeway has thousands of healthy products, including a wide range of organics, a sizable gluten-free section, natural sweeteners, and even pasture-raised chicken eggs and organic free-range meats right there alongside the Froot Loops. In fact, putting together a healthy diet is really one-stop shopping these days, with no need to schlep from store to store unless you want to.

One of the shifts that my family and I made when I changed my eating habits was no longer eating out on a regular basis. As I said earlier, I don't patronize big chain restaurants, and I find that the food at most restaurants just doesn't meet my standards. Much of it is delicious, I'm sure, but it usually fails to meet my other criteria: it must be healthy. So we eat at home, and I tease my husband about what a cheap date I am!

Theoretically, it doesn't need to cost anything to lose weight. After all, it doesn't cost more to eat less, right? But the reality is that most of us need help, and that help sometimes costs money. Whether that help is hiring a personal trainer, building a home gym, taking healthy-cooking classes, or even having weight-loss surgery, it's money well spent. After all, what's the cost of remaining trapped in the status quo?

IT'S TIME CONSUMING

My rock bottom experience shook me to the core. I quit my job impulsively; I felt like a failure professionally and personally, not just because of my job and my weight, but because I had failed even though I was trying so hard to do everything "right." It's bad enough when you've let yourself down, but when you feel as if you've disappointed those who love you the most, well, it was more than I could bear.

In the weeks and months that followed those desperate days, I was forced to confront a lot of hard truths. One of those truths was that I wasn't happy with how I spent my time.

Like most women, I had been pulled in more directions

I RAN ON THAT EMPTY TANK FOR AS LONG AS I COULD, BUT EVENTUALLY I HAD TO REFUEL. INVESTING TIME IN ACTIVITIES THAT MAKE ME HAPPY FILLS MY TANK.

than a ball of Silly Putty—work, volunteer activities, my kids, my husband, the house, even the dog! But in all that time I never once gave any thought to whether these activities made me happy. I mean, of course my children and my husband made me happy, but the activities that consumed me—how I made money, the organizations I gave my time to, and even my TV and Internet time—didn't give me pleasure.

I'm guessing you know that Silly Putty feeling: being pulled in a million different directions, always in reactive mode to the demands of your boss, your kids, your spouse, and all the other people who depend on you. But when I looked thoughtfully at those demands, I realized that at least some of it was unnecessary. As I started scaling back, I knew intuitively that engaging in activities that brought me joy and reorganizing my schedule was going to be an important part of this journey.

When I started setting my life back upright after my rock bottom, I had to confront a harsh reality: for years I had been chasing gratification with food because I was so dissatisfied with the way that I spent my time. I realized I was going to have to eliminate or at least pare down some of these dissatisfying activities if I had any chance of stopping this destructive cycle. Plus, how was I going to have time to shop for healthier food, learn new cooking techniques, plan and prepare food ahead of time, and exercise if I was always besieged with other people's demands? I knew I had to challenge every decision I made about how I spent my time.

I still had to work, of course. Not long after I broke down in my boss's office and quit my job impulsively, I took another paralegal job that was closer to home and was only four days a week rather than five. At the end of that school year I let go of all my volunteer commitments at my kids' schools and didn't sign on for any new ones for the coming year. I spent that summer really thinking about what would make me happy . . . not what *should* make me happy, but what time investments would actually make me happy.

I suppose you could argue that losing weight, in and of itself, isn't necessarily time consuming. If you think about it, it takes no more time to shop for healthy food than it does for unhealthy food. But of course planning and preparation do take time. As does exercise. I knew I couldn't just layer those important new habits on top of my already cram-packed life. As I set out on this new path, I wanted to build a life that was not only conducive to good health and weight loss, but also purposeful, meaningful, and full of just good plain fun!

It was a huge paradigm shift for me to allow myself to spend time doing things that weren't necessarily anybody's idea of productive, but were just things that I wanted to do. I was not raised to believe that I could ask for things just because I wanted them, let alone that I deserved them.

But what I learned as I stumbled into this new life is that I do deserve to be happy. It's okay to ask for the things I want—good health, physical fitness, personal accomplishment—and going after them is my right. So now I do. Do I feel twinges of guilt when I get e-mails about signing up for bake sales or chaperoning a school field trip? Yeah, but it passes. In fact, it passes pretty darn quickly when I'm out for a run on a beautiful sunny day.

I DON'T JUST GO ALONG TO GET ALONG ANYMORE.

Ultimately, the cost I paid for all of those activities I didn't enjoy was my own health. I ran on that empty tank for as long as I could, but eventually, I had to refuel. Investing time in activities that make me happy fills my tank.

These days I'm still busy, but in a very different way from the way I was before my weight loss. I work from home now, so I don't have a long commute to deal with anymore. I still work long hours, but I've discovered my passion for writing and helping other people find success. I make time for vigorous exercise six days a week now; that time is sacrosanct. I still chaperone the occasional school field trip, but I'll let somebody else sing in the church choir or bring cookies for the bake sale. (It's not good for my waistline anyway; I always eat the darn cookie dough!)

Prioritizing healthy living habits and reevaluating how I spent my time meant that I had to let go of many activities that were more obligatory than meaningful. When I did, it made room for healthy pursuits that now bring me so much joy.

IT CHANGES THE NATURE OF SOME RELATIONSHIPS

In each of our relationships, from our most casual to our most intimate, we fill a role for the other person. Of course, we're a husband or wife, father or mother, marketing manager or whatever the specific title is, but we're also a confidante, workout buddy, or maybe co-conspirator in unhealthy behaviors.

As supportive as people generally are, I've had my share of kinks to work out in my relationships. My PTA friends can't count on me to be the perpetual school volunteer anymore, stepping in to bring hot casseroles for teacher appreciation week (though I might offer to bring something healthy, if I've got time). And painful as it has been, there have been a few friendships that have not endured my transformation. As I said, in each of our relationships we fill a role for the other person; a few of my friendships were held up by our shared bad habits. When I veered away from dining at unhealthy restaurants and sharing fattening recipes, our friendships faded. It saddened me, but there seemed to be no middle ground, and we drifted apart. Fortunately, my remaining partners in crime and I will now just as likely go to an exercise class together as go shopping or get pedicures.

Now that I'm a rather public person in the realm of weight loss and healthy living, I meet lots of people who are committed to health and wellness at speaking engagements, through professional connections, and even via social media. For a woman whose Myers-Briggs classification is ISFJ (and in my case the *I*—for introvert—is both highlighted and underlined), this is quite an extraordinary turn of events. Earlier I mentioned that as my physical body got bigger, my world got smaller. An introvert by nature, my tendency to draw inward and isolate myself became extreme as I sought to avoid the public scrutiny and social interactions I found so humiliating. I'm very happy to report, though, that even though I still need time alone to work and recharge my batteries, I've found a whole new life in the company of supportive people who share my sunny outlook.

As wonderful as all of this is, I'm gonna be honest: the relationship that was the most challenging for me to deal with in terms of my new healthy-living agenda was with my husband. No, he's not one of those saboteurs we talked about earlier, and he's always been extremely supportive of my efforts to eat healthier and exercise. And I'd be lying if I said he wasn't pleased with my new shape. (Ahem, are there kids in the room?) But choosing to live differently has far-reaching ramifications. My new lifestyle hasn't just been about weight loss, it's been about living authentically. Learning to give voice to my own likes and dislikes and advocating for my passions means that I no longer just go along to get along.

Truthfully, this is one of the most challenging things we have encountered in our marriage—a marriage that is foundationally strong, thank goodness. Unraveling the complex emotions that were tied up in my unhealthy eating behavior meant I had to confront the deep-seated anger I felt toward my spouse. How could he not have seen how depressed I was? How could he just carry on with his life and career, seemingly blind to my suffering? All of that unraveling—some of it on our own, some of it in marriage counseling—left us both feeling rather wrung out.

YOUR BODY IS A REFLECTION OF WHAT YOU DO TO IT AND FOR IT EVERY DAY.

I will always be grateful to him for hanging in there with me while I figured out how to give voice to my deepest fears. Emotional intimacy with our most intimate partner—feeling genuinely known and accepted by them—is maybe the most fundamental emotional human need there is. It sounds so simple, but it requires tremendous vulnerability and trust. And though neither Rob nor I ever doubted our love or commitment to each other, it wasn't until I started dismantling my emotional eating that we came up against the barriers that we had both built up. Breaking them down took honesty, perseverance, and empathy.

Weight-loss surgery was the easy part, truly. The hard part for me has been figuring out what drove me to become obese in the first place and turning that around. Fortunately for me, with the patience and understanding of my husband, we're learning a new way of communicating. Almost thirty years into our marriage, we are stronger than ever. Our life together is based in deep trust and genuine emotional intimacy. I don't have to smile and wave anymore, feeling like a fraud. I am fully and authentically myself.

Though the road has been rocky at times, the price of change with regard to my relationships has been almost entirely positive. I may walk in slightly different social circles now, and there may be more people in those circles, but I've found so much support and encouragement in those connections.

And I'm never really certain if I'm just imagining it, but I think even my interaction with complete strangers is quite different from how it was when I was obese. I find I make eye contact more, I smile more, I share a thought or a joke more freely while waiting in line at Starbucks or at the grocery store. Being at peace with myself means that just walking through the world is a more pleasant experience, one that I am eager to share with everyone around me.

YOU NO LONGER GET TO HIDE BEHIND DENIAL, FEAR, MARTYRDOM, SELF-DOUBT, OR WHATEVER OTHER NEUROSES HAVE HELD YOU BACK

This may sound harsh. Certainly it's a big ol' serving of tough love with no holds barred. And the last thing I'm gonna say before I launch into it is that I made every one of these mistakes, to the *n*th degree, for decades. So the tough love comes from a place of deep understanding and compassion.

Okay, here goes.

Not only do I think you're in denial, I know you are. I was more than one hundred pounds overweight, and you don't get to be that heavy and not live in denial. You just don't. There's denial that you're gaining weight, there's denial that you're eating too much, and there's denial that your behavior is self-destructive. Truth is, your brain may be in denial, but your body is a reflection of what you do to it and for it every day. So your body's not in denial.

Your body reflects your reality.

Denial is powerful and devious; it manifests as rationalization, excuses, and justifications. It whispers all sorts of falsehoods in your ear. You find yourself making comparisons between yourself and others who seem to have advantages you do not: *Well, sure, if I had a chef (or a trainer . . . or a maid . . .) like she does, I'd eat well and work out every day.* Or you curse your bad luck, but make no plan to work around it: *If only I didn't have this bum knee I could run again, like I did in high school.* Or you cut yourself slack because it means you don't have to try as hard: *Well, I've had three kids so I'm never gonna have a slim waist again.* While it may be true that you don't have a bank account to rival Oprah's, or you have a bum knee, or your hormones have gone haywire, how does that give you license not to be the best you can possibly be *right now*? See your doctor, make a plan, giddyup, and let's go.

Fear will also undermine your weight-loss efforts. But, you wonder, *how could I be afraid of losing weight? I really, really want to lose weight!* It's not so much that you're afraid of losing weight; it's likely that you're afraid of confronting those issues that drive you to overeat. You're stressed out, overburdened, resentful, anxious, unsure, worried, uneasy, and feel trapped . . . maybe even depressed. So you turn to food as your tried-and-true method for easing those very uncomfortable feelings. And it helps you shut the feelings out for a while. But just like denial, fear is a destructive companion. To better understand your fear and help you face it, you may need an arsenal of tools: a doctor (to screen you for depression or other medical conditions), a therapist (to help you explore your situation and better understand what it is about your circumstances that makes you anxious, worried, and stressed out, and

167

to help you brainstorm workable solutions), a good friend (to provide a shoulder to lean on and an ear to bend), and maybe a little vitamin D in pill form—or better yet, sunshine. Don't underestimate the power of fresh air and sunshine on the old psyche. Exercise has a similar effect—imagine putting the two together, say every day at lunchtime, and you've got a powerful antidote to fear and anxiety.

Denial, anxiety, martyrdom, and self-doubt: they are crutches. You hobble along leaning on them because, as horrible as they feel, it's easier to lean on them than face whatever is causing them. The price of change is that you don't get to do that anymore. Continuing to do so will only keep you stuck right where you are.

This is some of the hardest work you will ever do in your life. Take baby steps. I am here to help you through this process, but you'll also need to assemble your own team. There's no special prize for doing it alone. Honestly, you know how I feel about this—doing it alone is a complete sham anyway because nobody does anything meaningful alone. Gather around you those people who can help you: doctors, friends, family, acquaintances who are a little ahead of you on the journey, random people you meet at the gym. People want to help; let them. Shining daylight on the feelings that you've been shoving down for years, if not decades, is difficult and scary. Don't try to do it alone.

As traumatic as my rock bottom experience was, I consider myself extremely lucky to have had it. While it left me shattered and humbled to the core, I was forced to surrender all of the labels I had held on to so tightly for decades: the perfect political wife, the doting mother, the diligent worker, the dedicated volunteer. My ego was dealt a harsh blow when I realized that all of those labels, and all of the energy I put into maintaining them, were just a façade. Likewise, all of the reasons (read: excuses) I told myself about why I couldn't improve my situation were blown to smithereens.

But it was also completely liberating. Choosing to proactively decide how to define success and happiness for myself, and to own the consequences of my own behavior, was revelatory and therapeutic for me. Living without excuses or denial is not just about banning cookies from the house, though— it's about making the kind of career and financial decisions that allow me to find happiness in my work and sleep soundly at night. It's about letting go of some people in my life who couldn't or didn't want to move in the same direction I was going. It's about refusing to be marginalized by some asinine 1950s stereotype of a political spouse because that's what people are comfortable with. It's about confronting or coming to terms with some of the dysfunctional relationships that I have carried with me since childhood.

Letting go of the excuses and fears that held me back has set me free. As difficult as this work has been, the cost—the money, time, friendships, and old ways of communicating in my marriage—has been mercifully low. Even so, no false modesty here—I have worked my ass off to earn my transformation. You may not have a sense yet of how high your price will be. Will you have to change jobs? Will some relationships be threatened? Certainly at a minimum you will have to carve out time in your schedule for healthy food prep and exercise. And there will be plenty of times when you'd much rather bury your head under the covers than rise early and head out into the cold to get your run in before your busy day starts. You must do a cost analysis of sorts, making a conscious decision to bear those costs in order to live a healthier life. This is exactly why I say that it takes a tremendous amount of courage to change your life. It's not that you necessarily have to be courageous to make good food choices or exercise. But surrendering those crutches we talked about and bearing the costs of changing the status quo takes the kind of grit we typically only ascribe to world-class athletes or intrepid explorers. Likely no one will ever chant our names in a stadium or plant a flag in our honor, but a steely determination is required to achieve our goals just the same.

And while there's no fame or fortune involved in self-discovery, the payoff is *huge*!

It's better than a big promotion at work or catching a foul ball in the seventh game of the World Series. It may even be better than scoring backstage passes at a Maroon 5 concert. (Hello, Adam Levine!) Permanent, lifelong weight loss—gaining a sense of mastery over something that has seemed impossible, finding hope and happiness where there had only been futility and misery—is like winning the Mega Millions jackpot! And it means that we'll never have to settle for anything less than our highest aspirations. Ever.

Chapter Eleven

TAKING THE LEAD: HOW I HELPED OTHERS BY HELPING MYSELF

A funny thing happens when you completely transform your life: people start looking to you for help
with their own struggles. As I said in chapter ten, as
I lost weight my world opened up as big as a Bloomin' Onion
at the Outback Steakhouse. Within a couple of years my cir-
cle of friends had grown significantly, but so had my role as
a leader within those circles. Without provocation from me,
friends and acquaintances would stop me at the gym to tell me
how they were stuck in a weight-loss plateau and ask for tips to
break through. Or they'd message me on social media, wanting to know how they could find the same spark of motivation that I had. I would talk to some for hours on the phone or
over coffee about their frustration with weight loss, the health

scares they'd encountered, and the obstacles they kept running up against as they attempted to change their lives. I could feel their heartache and desperation, feelings I know all too well.

As I struggled with figuring out the best way to share the knowledge that I'd gained about weight loss, I still had questions of my own. A couple of years into my own transformation I started running, a pursuit I threw myself into with tremendous enthusiasm, though relatively little information on how to go about it. I read a lot about running, but I also started asking people who I knew were runners for tips. I'd pester them with my unending questions, invite myself to go running with them, and just generally bother them ceaselessly as I talked through problems I encountered and revelations I wanted to share. I cannot even imagine how tiresome this must've been for them. Still, most of them were very patient with me and allowed me access to their wealth of knowledge. They encouraged me and gave me confidence along the way, and I am eternally grateful for their kindness and their patience.

The back-and-forth between these roles as both teacher and student has become a tremendously satisfying part of my weight-loss journey. It's an important concept that I referred to earlier as drafting. I'll talk a little bit more about it in this chapter too.

Closer to home, taking the lead has meant helping my son and my mother—both of whom had their own issues with obesity—transform their respective relationships with food. They each brought entirely different issues with regard to their eating patterns, their health history, and their reasons for having gained weight. They required different levels of oversight and input from me, but both of them were able to successfully identify a core reason why weight loss was important to them, and from that starting point we designed a plan to get them there. I'm so proud of them for achieving success, finding sustainable new habits, and maintaining their weight loss for several years.

When I set out on my own path to heal my lifelong struggle with my damaged self-esteem and to reform my distorted relationship with food, I had no idea that my healing would also inspire healing in those around me.

CONNOR'S STORY

My son Connor is a happy, healthy fifteen-year-old these days, if a little on the snarky side. (Gee, I wonder where he gets that?!? Ahem.)

Connor is the youngest of my four kids and has always been the pickiest eater of the bunch. When he was little, his tastes ran toward bland white foods—no sauces or spices of any kind. Not even ketchup or pepper! Like many parents, I allowed this behavior because it got him to eat, and it seemed the path of least resistance. I was a frazzled working mom, and the last thing I wanted when I finally walked in the door was a battle over what was on his dinner plate.

My older children had been picky as toddlers and pre-schoolers too, but, unlike his siblings, Connor's tastes weren't broadening as he got older. He basically subsisted on simple white carbs, fruit, and peanut butter. And he ate waaaaaaaaaaay too much of them. By age nine or ten, he was obese.

It wasn't until I came through my own weight-loss transformation that I realized the gravity of the situation. I felt terrible for having allowed this to happen. Connor was clearly unhappy, yet he was also extremely sensitive about his weight and his eating habits. Extended family members poked fun and made judgmental comments about his food choices. This made him painfully self-conscious, and he dreaded family gatherings.

When his eleven-year-old checkup approached I scheduled an appointment, but I also spoke to his pediatrician by telephone beforehand. "Here's what we're gonna do," I told the doctor. "You and I are gonna join forces and help this kid figure out a way to have a more balanced approach toward food." The doctor was completely supportive of my plan.

At the checkup, Connor's doctor ran through all the usual diagnostics, but he also opened a dialogue about how Connor felt about his weight and his eating habits. He showed us a chart of Connor's growth pattern, including a projection of his weight if we changed nothing. It wasn't good. Connor was already in the 95th percentile for weight (for his age, height, and gender), and the doctor was able to explain in a very matter-of-fact way how problematic it is to go through life as an overweight person. He asked Connor if he'd be willing to join a group ("along with mom!" he said) of kids and parents who were working on getting their weight back down into a normal range. Connor agreed. He wanted help.

Within a few weeks we started a sixteen-week program (through Group Health Cooperative in Seattle) that met weekly. The group was a cohort of a dozen or so families with a child (in some cases two) and at least one parent. The parent also had to be actively committed to losing weight and/or eating more healthfully. We were weighed privately each week and had to agree to attend all of the meetings for the duration of the class.

Connor and I each had a calorie range (based on our age, gender, and activity level) and activity goals we were to hit every day. We filled out food logs (old-school ones, on paper!) where we wrote down everything we ate, including the portion size, number of calories, and time of day eaten. We weighed, measured, and recorded everything we ate and drank every day throughout the sixteen-week class. No exceptions! We turned in those journals every week for evaluation by our facilitator. At the weekly meetings, the parents talked through challenges while the kids spent part of the time meeting separately with a nutritionist or staging and then running through an obstacle course or actively engaging in some other game.

Many positive things came out of this experience, but most

MY KIDS CAME TO EXPECT THEIR FOOD TO AMUSE AND ENTERTAIN THEM.

important, we learned that we were capable of taking charge of Connor's weight. During the group discussions, Connor was able to articulate why it was important to him to be a normal weight. At home, while we were measuring and weighing food in order to learn appropriate portion sizes, we were also learning to evaluate the calorie difference between a half cup of corn versus a half cup of green beans. (Hint, hint: if you have the green beans you save calories, which you can use toward dessert!)

And certainly, it's not that I didn't know that green beans are lower in calories than corn, it's just that I hadn't ever taken the time to talk to Connor about that. When we went to the grocery store or out to a restaurant, we looked at calorie counts and kept a running subtotal throughout the day. Connor learned that lower-calorie choices add up, and that making those choices consistently meant that he'd see the number on the scale go down the following week at our weigh-in. Rather than my nagging him (or him feeling guilty or confused), he felt empowered to make choices that were aligned with his goal: to lose weight.

All of this is to say, Connor came to *own* the decisions he made about food and exercise. In the months that followed, if I was away from the house at lunchtime on a Saturday, when I walked in the door I would find two tablespoons in the sink: one with peanut butter on it, one with jam on it. Connor had learned that you make a PBJ by measuring one tablespoon of each and spreading them on bread!

He had completely internalized the lessons learned in the class. He measured even when no one told him to. He measured because it mattered to him.

I am completely in awe of this kid.

Connor and I kept tracking his calories and activity even after the class was over because he hadn't quite hit his target weight yet. He'd weigh himself every few days on the scale in my bathroom early in the morning, and I'll never forget the morning he came running down the stairs with a huge grin on his face, jumping up and down, yelling, "Mommy, I'm normal!!!" What he meant, of course, is that his weight was in his target "normal" range. His excitement at his achievement was contagious, and I jumped up and down with him. He had found success!

Having grown up a fat kid myself—long before there were many fat kids—I know full well that being one is no fun. It's not just about aesthetics or being teased. It's not even just about better health (though being a normal weight almost always is healthier). And he certainly didn't have to lose weight to please my husband or me; we love Connor, and all of our kids, unconditionally. They don't have to earn it. It's their birthright. But I know how painful it is to feel like an outsider, never quite like everyone else. And I also know it doesn't just magically get better on its own. That class was my wake-up call that it was my responsibility, as his mom, to teach him what he needed to know about proper nutrition and how to respect his body.

And though most of us talk a pretty good talk about eating healthy food to our kids, in practice we often send mixed signals to our children. I was raised in this kind of environment, and it's one that I established with my own kids when I became a parent. I talked a lot about eating healthy foods, yet I had a shopping cart full of emotional eating issues of my own. As a result, I routinely brought unhealthy food home from the grocery store and served it to my family.

I'm the one who introduced them to Eggo waffles, SpongeBob-shaped macaroni and cheese, Go-Gurt, and lots of other "kid-friendly" foods. It certainly was not their fault that they came to see these foods as normal and expect them on their plates and in their lunch boxes. Likewise the same thing happened when we went out. The golden arches—or any of a number of other fast-food outlets—offered a quick, fun, on-the-go meal option. Plus a toy!

Even though I talked about eating healthy all the time, I created a food environment where food took on much more meaning than nourishment or even pleasure.

My kids came to expect their food to amuse and entertain them.

Just as I had been taught, I blindly schooled them on how food could "comfort" them, how it could satisfy their whim at any given moment.

Connor's unhappiness about his weight shook me to the core. I felt terrible for having neglected to guide him toward a healthier way of eating, but once I realized my mistake I worked quickly; with the help of his pediatrician and the program Connor and I attended together, we were able to turn his eating habits around.

There are two important reasons why Connor's experience was so dramatically divergent from my own childhood experience, when I was dropped off at that Weight Watchers meeting so many years before.

- Connor and I went through the program together. The program itself was geared toward kids his age (they were all within a few years of one another). There were no mixed messages; Connor and I were on the same page and in it together. Over a period of months we completely changed the food culture of our entire family. There wasn't "Mom's and Connor's food" and everybody else's food; there was just good, healthy food.

- The pediatrician and the program facilitator took a matter-of-fact approach that was nonjudgmental. I learned to give Connor choices within his calorie range each day so that he could evaluate those choices on his own. For example, one day early in the program he and I were at the grocery store when we decided we'd do a side-by-side comparison of tortillas. I'd always told him that he "should" eat whole-wheat tortillas rather than the white-flour ones he preferred, because I assumed they were healthier. But he didn't like the whole-wheat ones, and getting him to eat them was like pulling teeth. So we stood there in the grocery aisle, he and I, comparing the nutritional information on the packages. Turns out the whole-wheat tortillas have one additional gram of fiber and only ten fewer calories than the white ones. I was astonished. I threw the whole-wheat tortillas back on the shelf and said (a little too loudly), "Screw it! If you like the white ones better, let's just get the white ones!" Connor smiled and said, "Ask me how much I love the fact that I have the kind of mom who will say 'screw it!' at the grocery store." Ultimately, we compromised by making Connor's favorite cheese quesadillas out of one white-flour tortilla rather than two, as we had always done previously. Fewer calories.

He made the choice.
He owned the solution.
Pure. Freaking. Genius.

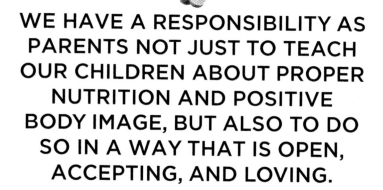

WE HAVE A RESPONSIBILITY AS PARENTS NOT JUST TO TEACH OUR CHILDREN ABOUT PROPER NUTRITION AND POSITIVE BODY IMAGE, BUT ALSO TO DO SO IN A WAY THAT IS OPEN, ACCEPTING, AND LOVING.

I learned that the best approach is to educate and inspire my children, lead by example, communicate positive and consistent messages about healthy living, and offer ample opportunities to eat healthy and exercise together as a family.

What I don't do is bring unhealthy food into our home and then hover over them, wagging my finger at them, telling them they "shouldn't eat that." Good grief.

Creating a hostile food environment full of conflicting messages doesn't prevent children from overeating; it teaches them that the adults in their life cannot be trusted in this regard. It drives their food choices underground. It instills fear, guilt, and shame. It is devastating on every level.

Not a living soul ever lost a pound (not permanently, anyway) out of fear, guilt, or shame. No adult, nor any child.

My son learned something that it took me until my midforties to figure out: you must have your own *internal* reason why living healthfully is important. That is the only way it works.

MY MOM'S STORY

Raise your hand if you have an uncomplicated relationship with your mother.

So nobody, right? Yeah, me either.

This is one of the most complex human relationships there is. For those of us who are lucky enough to have our mothers in our lives, we may still struggle with some of the lingering issues from childhood, or fall back into the parent-child roles we know so well. My relationship with my own mother has been as tumultuous as they come. In my formative years I came to believe that manic dieting, emotional eating, and self-loathing due to a distorted body image were normal. Food was a weapon of mass destruction in my childhood home, and the fallout wasn't pretty.

My mother spent her entire adult life—up until a few years ago—going up and down the dieting roller coaster. Frankly, I don't remember her ever being happy with her weight, even when she was thin by all reasonable standards. In recent years she's shared with me much of what went on in her own childhood home, and I've come to be much more sympathetic now that I know what she endured. Her suffering reinforces my belief that we have a responsibility as parents not just to teach our children about proper nutrition and positive body image, but also to do so in a way that is open, accepting, and loving. Children want nothing more than their parents' love and approval. If a child can only achieve that by driving his or her own needs and desires underground, then that's exactly what they'll do.

A few years after I started losing weight, my mother was telling me over the phone about how she was just about to start a new diet, but she had to wait because one of her friend's birthdays was in a few days, and they were going to go out. On my end of the phone I'm smacking my forehead because I can't believe she's still doing this.

In my typical sympathetic manner I said, "Mom, what the heck are you doing? Why do you do this???" There is no conceivable way my exasperation wasn't evident in my voice.

"Do what?" she asked obliviously.

"Why do you delay making better food choices simply because you're gonna go out with your girlfriends? It's like you think you've gotta get all you can before you sentence yourself to some horrible new diet. It's self-torture. And unfortunately, I know exactly how it's all going to play out too; it's gonna end in a flurry of chocolate-chip-cookie-dough ice cream! Why don't you let me show you how *I* eat? It's a way that you can eat every day, whether you're going out with your friends or not."

There was silence on the other end of the phone. Uh-oh. Did I go too far?

"I'll write up a schedule for you, bring you some of the foods that I eat every day, and we'll talk through how it might work for you. Would that be okay?"

"Sure," Mom said. "I'll give it a go."

Mom likes to tell the story about how we met the next day at Panera Bread over a bowl of their black-bean soup. (Have you had it? It's fab. But skip the roll.) I showed up with two grocery bags full of the kinds of foods I eat regularly: steel-cut oats, my scrumptious Vegan Thumbprint cookies (see recipes section), almond milk, avocados, arugula, and lots more goodies.

"See, Mom," I said as I showed her my Food Blueprint, "you eat five to six times a day, small meals comprised mostly of lean protein and lots of vegetables."

"Do I get to have yogurt?" she asked.

"Yes! But switch to nonfat Greek yogurt. It has more protein and less sugar than that fake stuff with the fruit already mixed in. Instead, mix in your own fresh fruit and maybe some slivered almonds or chopped walnuts."

"What about dessert?" she wanted to know. I think having a sweet tooth is a genetic marker on our DNA. Runs in the family.

"Yes, you can have dessert if you want to, but it really just depends on whether or not you leave enough calories at the end of your day. Also, hold it to no more than 150 calories, and even better if it's from a naturally sweet source, like fresh or dried fruit, or a sugar-free sorbet."

"Huh," she said, ruminating. "That sounds easy enough. It's certainly worked well for you."

I'm only recounting one pivotal conversation here, but the truth is that my mother had been watching my transformation closely for the preceding three or four years. After having yo-yo dieted her entire life, she was ready for her own lifestyle makeover. When she committed to changing her eating habits, it was because she'd witnessed my success firsthand, and she saw how my new habits had helped me gain control over the demon that had tormented us both for so long.

But before I make it sound like it was all rainbows and unicorns, let me say that Mom and I had a serious discussion at that Panera Bread about her tendency to give herself "outs." Because she's retired and she's very social, Mom has lots of friends that she meets regularly for coffee or lunch. She'd do the "last supper" kind of behavior like I described above, where she'd start a very restrictive diet only after bingeing with her friends or over the holidays. I can't tell you how many times she's told me, "I was doing so great on my diet, but it was so-and-so's birthday, and she wanted to go to Applebee's . . ." Now, if anyone other than my mom had said that to me I might have been a little more diplomatic, but with my own family I'm about as subtle as a sledgehammer.

"Mom, it's *always* gonna be somebody's birthday. You're *always* going to be meeting friends for coffee or whatever. We have to help you figure out a way that you can go out with your friends and be social and still stick to your Food Blueprint. You wanna know what I think?" I added (speaking rhetorically, because of course I was gonna tell her).

She nodded tentatively.

BESIDES ALL THE USUAL STUFF I LEARNED FROM MY MOM, I ALSO LEARNED THAT IT'S NEVER TOO LATE TO WANT SOMETHING BETTER FOR YOURSELF.

"I think you're using your social engagements as an excuse to indulge. You know full well you could make better food choices, even at the places you and your friends like to go. You could choose lower-calorie foods at those same restaurants, and you could reduce your portion size by about half and take the other half home. You're not doing it because, on some level, you don't want to do it."

"You're right," she said. "But I do want to do it. I'm tired of living this way."

Before I sent her on her way, Mom and I used one of the online calculators to figure out her basal metabolic rate (the rate at which the body uses energy while at rest to keep vital functions going, such as breathing and keeping warm).

Knowing my mom's penchant for highly restrictive dieting, I said, "Don't ever, *ever* eat fewer calories than that in a day, okay? If you do, your body will go into starvation mode, and it slows your metabolism down. That's exactly the opposite of what we want to do. It's counterproductive, so don't do it."

"Okay," she agreed.

Then, based on her basal metabolic rate and her activity level (at the time it was sedentary to light), we added in about 250 to 300 calories to come up with a calorie target for her to hit each day. And with that, she left with two bags of groceries, a Food Blueprint, and a newfound resolve to care for herself in a whole new way.

We talked by phone every few days—it really does help to talk to someone who understands the temptations and the struggles—but she required relatively little oversight from me. Like most of us lifetime dieters, she's an expert on how many calories are in nearly everything. Over the course of the first few weeks she made changes to my Food Blueprint, adding her own favorite healthy foods here, removing some of mine that she didn't care for there. That's the beauty of the Food Blueprint; it's meant to be a formula into which you plug your own preferences. By choosing foods that worked with her lifestyle, Mom could customize it so that all of the foods in her Food Blueprint met the two criteria to be on her table: they are healthy, and she absolutely loves them, thus making it easier for her to stick with the program.

One month into her new eating plan, Mom lost five pounds.

"Huh," she said to me over another bowl of soup. Curried lentil this time.

"That wasn't so hard. I think I'll do it again."

So she did. The next month she lost another five pounds. Then another.

After about a year, she'd lost just over seventy pounds. At age seventy-plus, my mother lost about 40 percent of her body weight. Maybe more important, she feels like she's gained a sense of mastery over something that she'd felt a slave to her whole life. Just like me, after she'd lost most of her weight she felt so much better both physically and mentally that she began exercising. Mom lives close to a senior center that offers free use of exercise equipment, so she goes over there several times a week to walk on the treadmills. When the weather's nice she walks outside, even walking to run errands instead of driving.

Taking better care of herself has meant that Mom also gets to her doctor regularly when she encounters problems, rather than brushing things off as part of the aging process. Mom's got her share of aches and pains, and she's learned that being active means she's got to stay on top of her self-care if she wants to remain so. Now we run that 12K race together that I mentioned earlier—in our hometown of Spokane, Washington (Bloomsday)—every spring. It's a great tradition that we enjoy tremendously, and can I just say that when we cross that finish line, we are both on top of the world!

Besides all the usual stuff I learned from my mom, I also learned that it's never too late to want something better for yourself. Above all else, the biggest determining factor in whether you're successful at weight loss is your own belief that you deserve something better. It's never too late to embark on a new path.

My mom taught me that.

DRAFTING

I didn't do very well in my high school physics class, but here's drafting in a nutshell: Drafting is a physical phenomenon whereby both the leader and the follower in a group of moving objects gain an advantage from their interdependence. The follower can go faster, with less effort, because the leader is moving air out of the way and is essentially "pulling" him or her along. The leader also gets a "push" from the airflow of the follower. In chapter five I talked about drafting in the context of pulling in behind those who are ahead of you on the weight-loss journey.

Without realizing I was drafting, I utilized this exact strategy when I started running. I had a lot more enthusiasm than actual knowledge, and as excited as I was to learn more, there was a steep learning curve I had to run up. There's a lot more to running than I learned in my middle school PE classes: there is hills training and HIIT (high-intensity interval training), there is proper nutrition and injury prevention, there is racing and recovery. Besides all the reading I did, I wanted to learn first-hand from runners about the mistakes they made, the insights they had, and the tips and secrets they were willing to share. The knowledge I gained and the support these new friends offered has been invaluable.

I think of weight loss as a similar road. Rather than travel the road alone, expending maximum effort, I like to join the pack.

Living a healthy lifestyle can sometimes feel like swimming upstream, and I'll admit that sometimes I feel a little out of step with what's "normal" in our culture: I don't eat much of the mass-marketed processed or restaurant foods that most people eat. But I've found support in like-minded new friends and online sources that offer inspiration and information. As

I reach out for reinforcement, others are reaching back and offering a helping hand in my quest for living a healthy lifestyle. Through them I've found new restaurants and recipes to try, new exercise classes to attend, and even new workout buddies. There are times I'm now in a position to do this for someone who is just a little bit behind me on the journey. I find that both as the follower and the leader, I benefit tremendously from these relationships.

As you travel your own road to better health, you too will encounter others who are either ahead or behind you on the same road. When you meet someone who's a little ahead of you, pull in behind. Emulate what they're doing; ask questions about their eating and exercise habits. Let them help you.

As you have success in accomplishing your healthy-living goals people will reach out to you for encouragement and support. Extend a hand to them and teach them what you've learned.

Whether it's in fitness or in weight loss, we all do better when we support one another. In fact, I'd go so far as to say that I believe that's what we're all called to do during our very limited time here on earth: help each other out along the way. As for me, I spent enough years too afraid and ashamed to ask for help. Now I love to ask for help; it's like opening the windows on the first warm day in spring to let the fresh air in. And when I have the opportunity to be that breath of fresh air for someone else, I feel more blessed than I ever could have imagined.

When you get a chance, be that breath of fresh air for someone else; create a draft zone behind you. There's power in numbers, and together we're unstoppable!

Chapter Twelve

SPREADING THE MESSAGE: CHANGING OUR LIVES SO WE CAN CHANGE THE WORLD

Fundamentally, overeating and dieting are two sides of the same coin; both can be self-destructive. I bounced back and forth between the two for as long as I can remember until I decided to try a different path.

The profound realization I had when my world came crashing down around me—that I was worth fixing—was life changing for me. In an instant I recognized that whether I was standing in my pantry stuffing down food in an effort to numb pain, or punishing myself by going on yet another highly restrictive diet, I'd spent a lifetime beating myself up for not measuring up to some mythical ideal. Committing to changing my behavior forever was quite simply an acknowledgment that beating myself up was unnecessary, because there wasn't

HEALTHY LIVING IS REALLY JUST SELF-LOVE.

anything wrong with me. Taking care of myself was validation that I was inherently valuable and that I deserved to be treasured. It was an appreciation for this incredible gift I've been given—my life and my health. The work I do now to maintain my good health I do with a grateful heart. I guess what I came to know over time is that healthy living is really just self-love.

Now, I wouldn't for a minute presume that everybody who is overweight or obese has self-esteem issues, though I believe many of us are emotional eaters. And remember, emotional eating, at its most basic level, is denial. Part of self-love, I believe, has to include being willing to accept every part of ourselves—the good, the bad, and the half gallon of Ben & Jerry's that calls to us in the middle of the night. To succeed, you play to your strengths and manage your weaknesses. For me that means the Ben & Jerry's has to go.

But how do we do this on a bigger scale? How do we apply that principle of self-love to our nation's obesity crisis? What would that look like in terms of solving childhood obesity? Is it possible for us to turn our dire situation around, or have we already passed the point of no return?

If you or a family member are suffering, or you share my concern about our nation's and our children's health, you have reason to be concerned. But I believe that there is also cause for optimism. As individuals, as families, and as members of our broader communities, there are many reasons to have hope that our future is not yet determined. In fact, I believe there are a thousand reasons.

1,000 CAUSES, 1,000 SOLUTIONS

Just as there are probably a thousand causes of obesity, I believe there must also be a thousand solutions. That is to say, the problem of obesity is complex and multilayered: we have created a Standard American Diet that is overloaded with processed foods and laden with chemicals that quite likely interfere with hormonal regulators; we live hectic, stressful lives where many feel so trapped in jobs they hate that overindulging in unhealthy food becomes a substitute for the satisfaction they crave; and we have engineered most physical exertion out

ULTIMATELY WE GET EXACTLY THE SOCIETY WE DESERVE.

of our lives, leaving us sedentary and detached from our physical bodies. Whether it's by neglect or default, our national waistband is expanding at an alarming rate, with 69 percent of adult Americans now either overweight or obese. (For more information on the crisis of obesity in America, go to www.cdc.gov/nchs/fastats/obesity-overweight.htm.)

It will take time, money, political will, public awareness, and grassroots activism to change directions. What's absolutely clear is there won't be a one-plus-size-fits-all solution to obesity. And while there may indeed be medical advances in the treatment of obesity, the solution will not be found in a magic pill formulated in a medical research facility. Likewise, there is plenty of room at the solutions table for federal, state, and local agencies, but there will be no sweeping governmental program sent to rescue us from ourselves.

Those thousand solutions I speak of will come in myriad forms: improved school lunch programs that offer whole foods instead of processed ones; community-based outreach programs and programs run by nonprofits that teach cost-effective ways to shop for healthy food and cooking skills to low-income families; and reduced government subsidies for certain crops, which artificially lower their cost, making them cheap ingredients for food manufacturers.

The public awareness and grassroots activism that I talk about is us: you and me. We are an integral part of the thousand solutions, with roles to play within our families and as members of our broader communities. Author, activist, and poet Maya Angelou encouraged us to do the best we can until we know better; then when we know better, we must do better. It's up to us to do better. We owe it to our children, and we deserve nothing less for ourselves. To bring about that change, though, we must join our voices and make ourselves heard.

We make ourselves heard on this issue in a thousand ways: by speaking up at PTA and school board meetings where decisions are made about school nutrition policies and physical education programs, by electing leaders who prioritize their constituents' health over big agriculture's interests, and by patronizing local businesses that support community-based health and wellness. The long and the short of it is this: our choices matter. How we choose to spend our money and our time reflects our personal and family values. If we value healthy living, then we must invest time and energy into leveraging our everyday choices to that end. (Hint, hint: while that still allows for going out with coworkers for happy hour on Friday after work, it doesn't involve ordering the super macho nachos or the megasized strawberry-kiwi margarita. Sorry.) Our everyday choices affect our own health, but they also help shape the society in which we live.

Ultimately, we get exactly the society we deserve. If we make our voices heard on healthy-living issues that matter to us within our circles of influence, if we leverage our purchasing power as consumers by shopping for products and services that are aligned with our values, and if we speak our opinions openly in the public arena, we can bring about the cultural changes we want to see.

But not every change needs to be on a grand scale. An important part of those thousand solutions are our closer-to-home choices that affect our immediate lives.

For example, one simple closer-to-home solution is to raise the issue of birthday treats in our children's classrooms. Certainly we want to celebrate each child's special day in school, and there's absolutely nothing wrong with bringing a healthy snack to share, but maybe you're not the only parent who's counting up how many grams of sugar your child is consuming each time a classmate brings in a box of doughnuts or cupcakes on a birthday. Bring up the issue at curriculum night to see if you can raise awareness and support for celebrating birthdays in healthier ways. Similarly, parents pass around the snack sign-up sheet at the start of each sports season to make sure their team is well fueled. Problem is, those snacks often are highly processed and loaded with sugar (or salt or high fructose corn syrup). I'll bet you anything that if you speak up and suggest that snacks consist of unprocessed whole fruits and veggies and water, you'll see a lot of the other parents nodding their heads in agreement.

Being mindful of calories and establishing good eating habits isn't just a concern for the parents of overweight children; we're setting all of our kids' eating behaviors and taste buds for life. It's vital we teach them the best way to fuel their bodies while their palates are still emerging. Of course the occasional sugary treat is fine, but when they're so commonplace that kids

EAT LIKE IT MATTERS

consume them daily, they're no longer special, and kids' palates become accustomed to them. Through parental awareness and positive role modeling, we can begin to change our kids' expectations that unhealthy food is a reward or comfort.

These closer-to-home solutions are everywhere in our everyday world. Just last December I walked into my YMCA one morning to find a bake sale going on in the lobby. I was upset about the mixed message this sends to members who look at our Y as another one of our safe havens, just like we create in our homes. This is supposed to be a place of health and wellness, and, in my opinion, you don't kick those values to the curb just because you're raising money for something. Even if it's for a good cause! I took my frustration to the director of membership and explained why I felt that a bake sale was completely inappropriate. He agreed, and said that he'd just never thought of it that way before. I suggested that we brainstorm other ways for groups to fundraise and offered to contact the executive director about making a policy change. It isn't that I think bake sales are inherently evil, it's just that we're surrounded by unhealthy foods everywhere we go; maybe it's okay for us to ask that this place, which is so much more than a gym—it's really a community of health-minded people, be free from the temptations we face everywhere else.

Obesity's thousand solutions include everything from national wellness campaigns like First Lady Michelle Obama's Let's Move! initiative, to the deeply personal decisions we each face as individuals, and everything in between. Whether our actions are on a grand scale or a private one, the responsibility to care for our children, our nation, and ourselves lies with each one of us. This new "American Revolution" will begin in our kitchens and will be fought with our dollars, our hearts, and our indomitable spirit.

WHY EATING LIKE IT MATTERS IS
PART OF LIVING LIKE IT MATTERS

When people ask me why I decided to write about my struggle with my weight, I tell them that sometimes I secretly wish I could just sit down and shut up about it. Truly, I find it embarrassing to talk about my food demons, my unhappiness in my marriage and my home life, my failure in my career, and my inability to control my weight.

But as difficult as it is for me to talk publicly about my struggles, I know that there are lots of people who share my pain. And not to sound immodest, but I've learned a lot about how successful lifelong weight loss works. Maybe most important, I've learned that I can find success even though I am still a deeply flawed, far-from-perfect human being. I am moved to share my story and my insight with others so that we might walk this path together.

UNLESS A BEAR IS CHASING YOU, FEAR IS A POOR MOTIVATOR.

Moving forward, I plan to be an active voice in the public arena, talking about how we can shift to a healthier approach to our eating habits. After years of hiding from the spotlight of political life, I've now found my own reason to stand at the podium, as a leader. To keep my personal goals in the forefront of my life, I like to emphasize non-scale-related goals. Staying real about my weight means, for me, weighing myself three times per week (first thing in the morning, after I pee and exhale deeply). But I always like to be working toward something specific, not just a number on the scale. I find that having a tangible goal (usually a race, in my case) keeps me focused on something I want to accomplish. Striving to see a certain number on the scale has never been helpful for me; it makes me anxious, and I find myself reacting out of fear. Unless a bear is chasing you, fear is a poor motivator. As soon as the initial fear wears off, poof! There goes your motivation.

Besides, I don't define success by a number on the scale; I define it by how I feel. Am I happy? Do I feel a sense of satisfaction in my work and in my home life? Am I proud of what I did that day as my head hits the pillow each night? If I can answer those questions with a resounding *Yes!* then I am successful.

The three things that I asked you to commit to at the beginning of this book—to dig deep, to create a vision for yourself, and to embrace change—are really just the beginning. And the truth is, even though we've got a good solid start, there is no finish line. Despite what the diet programs, weight-loss books, and infomercials promise, we won't ever "lose the weight for good." As if somehow we do it once, wipe our hands of it, and we're done.

Healthy living is a daily commitment.

We eat like it matters because it's a part of living like it matters. Living like it matters also means working, moving, learning, teaching, leading, and loving like it matters. It all matters because we matter. And we don't just matter because people depend on us. Or even because our families love us. We matter because, I believe, we each have a purpose in life. My own journey began with the very humble realization that, even though I may not have known on those very dark days what that purpose was, I knew at the core of my being that my purpose wasn't to be miserable for the rest of my life. I felt—in a visceral way—that my life was meant for so much more than I could see from that vantage point.

YOU ARE THE GAME CHANGER IN YOUR OWN LIFE.

I may have set out on a weight-loss journey, but what I found was a whole new way to be. I came to realize that happiness on my terms is possible. And, of course, I also found that weight loss is possible. Whether you're eleven years old, like my son was, seventy-plus years young, like my mom, or pushing the upper limits of middle age, like me, *transformative change* is possible.

YOU ARE THE GAME CHANGER: IT'S GO TIME!

You've probably tried to lose weight dozens, if not hundreds, of times before. You think about it every day. But you wonder if you can summon the courage to try again. I'm gonna let you in on a little secret: you can. In fact, not only can you summon the necessary courage to try again, you have the power to make your wildest dreams come true. But in addition to that courage, you're gonna need to pack one more item in your rucksack before you go on your way: curiosity. Bring your curiosity with you on this journey as you explore which weight-loss plan works best for you; it might be my Food Blueprint, it might be weight-loss surgery, or it might be something else entirely. Be willing to question the assumptions you hold about your own limitations. Be inquisitive when meeting new people, especially those whose passions you find intriguing. The eagerness you bring to your task will go a long way in helping you deal with the inevitable obstacles and challenges that will come up along the way. Let your courage strengthen your resolve, and let your curiosity fuel your drive.

You are the game changer in your own life.

You're ready to do this now; I know it. Do it because you want to feel better. Do it because you can't stop thinking about it. Do it because you want to discover your true potential. Do it because you deserve nothing less.

The bottom line is that you and I deserve the very best that life has to offer; it is our birthright. But nobody is going to hand it to us; we've gotta go after it every single day, with everything we've got.

Losing weight is hard, maybe the hardest thing you'll ever do. But it gets easier, I swear it does. And you're so damn worth it.

Let's go get it!

Recipes

FUEL-THE-DAY BREAKFASTS

* * * * * * * * * * *

When we "eat like it matters," we start the day strong by giving our bodies the best possible fuel. I like to front-load my calories by taking in more in the early part of the day, then tapering toward the evening. It may seem counterintuitive, but research (and my own experience) shows that front-loading staves off cravings later in the day.

We may only get one chance to make a first impression, but each day we've got the opportunity to be our best selves. And naturally, that starts with breakfast!

METABOLIC DETOX TEA

I went through a difficult time when menopause took hold. After my regular gynecologist exhausted her bag of tricks and I saw no relief from my symptoms, I enlisted the help of a natu- ropath. She put me on a brutal detox elimination diet for six weeks; the roughest part may have been weaning myself off caffeine. As she and I discussed, I'd been riding a roller coaster of energy highs and lows throughout the day, and because I'm busy and don't have time to be exhausted several times a day, she banished from my diet my two go-to pick-me-ups: caffeine and sugar (though mercifully, a small amount of natural sugar from honey, pure maple syrup, and fruit was allowed).

This tea was my answer to my early morning foggy head. I drink this energizing detox tea every morning now and feel so much better. Don't get me wrong; detoxing from caffeine was tough. But now that I'm off I can see how the caffeine-sugar roller coaster was messing with my energy level and moods all day long. Try this tea first thing every morning when you wake up. It's a gentle, soothing way to start your day.

INGREDIENTS:

- 1/2 cup organic honey
- 4 tsp ground ginger
- 2 tsp ground turmeric
- 1 dash cayenne pepper
- 2 pinches black pepper
- Lemon juice and lemon zest* (see note below)

DIRECTIONS:

Combine honey, ginger, turmeric, cayenne, and black pepper in a small jar; whisk until ingredients are well mixed. Refrigerate.

*Rather than zest and juice a half lemon each morning, I zest and juice 6 to 8 lemons at a time, and divide the zest and juice equally into an ice cube tray. I freeze it, and then transfer the frozen cubes to a zip-top bag. Each little cube is the perfect amount for one cup of tea, and has the added benefit of cooling my tea just enough so it's drinkable right away.

Into a mug, combine one heaping teaspoon of the honey mixture and a frozen lemon "ice cube." Steep mixture with boiling water, stirring until well combined. Enjoy!

MARILYN'S FIRST-THING-IN-THE-MORNING "LET'S-GO-GET-IT!" SMOOTHIE

You might think I'd get tired of drinking this smoothie (almost) every day for breakfast for the past several years, but I don't. Each morning I look forward to it; it's sweet and satisfying, and I love the flavor combination. But feel free to mix it up and try different fruits that suit your taste (hint, hint: kiwi is a delicious substitute for mango). The chia and ground flaxseeds give it fiber, antioxidants, and omega-3s for an added boost.

Please note that this smoothie's pretty high in calories (420), so I only use it as my preworkout fuel. Makes one serving.

INGREDIENTS:

- 1/2 frozen banana
- 2/3 cup frozen mango
- 8 oz nonfat plain Greek yogurt
- 1 tbsp raw, unfiltered, organic apple cider vinegar (it helps control blood sugar and aids digestion)
- 1 packet Emergen-C drink mix (any flavor)
- 1 tbsp chia seeds
- 2 tbsp ground organic flaxseeds
- 1-1/2 cups very cold water

DIRECTIONS:

Place ingredients in blender; mix well. Enjoy!

BADASS GREEN
PROTEIN SMOOTHIE

I finally came up with a green smoothie that is healthy *and* tastes good! The secret is to use frozen kale plus banana and mango, which are super sweet. The result is a smoothie that is nutritious and filling, but even better, it's creamy and delicious! Use it before or after your tough workout to fuel up or recover. Makes one serving.

INGREDIENTS:

- 1 scoop vanilla protein powder
- 1 packet orange-flavored Emergen-C
- 1 tbsp ground flaxseeds
- 1 tbsp raw, unfiltered, organic apple cider vinegar
- 1/2 frozen banana
- 2/3 cup frozen mango chunks
- 1/2 cup frozen kale
- 1-1/2 cups very cold water

DIRECTIONS:

Place ingredients in blender and power up your day! Enjoy!

LUNCH
FAVORITES

* * * * * * * *

I may very well be the laziest (healthy) cook in North America.

I don't know about you, but when faced with typical weight-loss menu plans that insist on my making something different for breakfast, lunch, and dinner each day, my inner four-year-old emerges, hands on hips, and shouts, "You're not the boss of me!" How mature. Ahem.

I'm a path-of-least-resistance shopper and a lazy cook. I want to make one thing—I must *love* it and it must be *healthy*—for lunch and enjoy it every day for the week. It simplifies my life, makes weight loss easier, and tames my inner four-year-old. So there.

LENTIL TOMATO SOUP

It seems natural that this warm, inviting soup would be a winter favorite. After all, it's rich and hearty, with enough spice to make it interesting. But the truth is, I love it all year long. I make it on a Sunday, have it for lunch each day that week, then freeze the other half for another week. This recipe never fails to deliver a bowlful of wonderfulness every time I dip my spoon in. Makes ten servings.

INGREDIENTS:

- 2 cups chopped onion
- 1 tsp ground turmeric
- 1 tsp ground cumin
- 1 tsp chili powder
- 1 tsp red pepper flakes
- 1/4 tsp salt
- 1/4 tsp black pepper
- 2 garlic cloves, minced
- 3-1/3 cups water
- 2-1/3 cups dried lentils (regular or red), rinsed
- 1/3 cup fresh cilantro, chopped
- 3 – 14.5-oz cans fat-free, low-sodium chicken broth (or vegetable broth, if preferred)
- 1 – 28-oz can diced tomatoes, undrained
- Chopped fresh tomatoes (for optional garnish)
- Cilantro sprig (for optional garnish)

DIRECTIONS:

Coat a large Dutch oven with olive oil cooking spray and heat to medium-high. Add the onion; sauté for 3 minutes or until tender. Add the turmeric, cumin, chili powder, red pepper flakes, salt, pepper, and garlic; sauté for 1 minute. Add water, lentils, cilantro, chicken broth, and diced tomatoes. Bring to a boil. Reduce heat and simmer for one hour.

Reserve 2 cups of the lentil mixture. Using an immersion blender, puree the soup until smooth. Stir in the reserved 2 cups of the lentil mixture. Garnish with chopped tomatoes and cilantro, if desired.

SPICY BLACK-BEAN SOUP

"Hi, my name is Marilyn, and I have a Spicy Black-Bean Soup problem."

Oh, sorry. That's the way we start our 12-step group meetings. (I'm joking.)

I am addicted to this stuff. But what a way to go, right?! Here's the thing: not only is the soup itself fabulous, but you can top it with all the same stuff you love on tacos (in very small amounts, please; these are garnishes after all). It's so delicious and so healthy, there's no reason not to eat it every day.

I'll save you a seat at our next meeting. Makes ten servings.

INGREDIENTS:

- 1 tbsp olive oil
- 2 cups pico de gallo (see recipe on page 223)
- 1 tbsp ground cumin
- 1 tsp salt
- 1/2 tsp pepper
- 4 – 15-oz cans black beans, rinsed and drained
- 2 – 14.5-oz cans of diced fire-roasted tomatoes (such as RO*TEL), not drained
- 1 – 4-oz can minced jalapeños
- 1 – 32-oz box vegetable broth (or chicken broth, if you prefer)
- Juice of half a lime

OPTIONAL GARNISHES:

- Diced cilantro

- Plain nonfat Greek yogurt
- Avocado
- Shredded sharp cheddar
- Pico de gallo

DIRECTIONS:

Heat olive oil in Dutch oven. Add most of the pico de gallo (reserving a small amount for optional garnish), cumin, salt, and pepper. Heat thoroughly, about 3 to 5 minutes. Add three cans of the rinsed and drained beans, the two cans of tomatoes, and the can of jalapeños and heat through. Add vegetable broth and bring to low boil. Reduce heat, cover, and simmer, about 10 minutes. Use an immersion blender to mostly puree the soup. Add the remaining can of black beans and the lime juice. Heat through. Serve with cilantro or any of the other garnishes. Enjoy!

SIMPLE
SNACKS

* * * *

Managing hunger is a critical part of weight loss. The best way to manage hunger is to eat satisfying, healthy meals and snacks every 2 to 3 hours. Doing so has the added benefit of maintaining steady blood sugar and keeping your metabolism burning.

Snacks needn't be complicated or time consuming; in fact, the best ones don't require a recipe! My snacks are often as simple as a handful of cashews and an apple, or a hard-boiled egg and veggies.

When I do invest the time to make a more sophisticated snack, it's gotta be something really special. These three are worth the time.

There is no better reward after a tough workout than my Peanut Butter & Jelly Smoothie. With four ingredients, it comes together in a snap, and it gives me my PBJ fix in a super-healthy and satisfying way. (But no extra dipping into the jar of peanut butter with a spoon!)

I'm not even sure my Whole-Grain Wrap Veggie "Pizza" counts as a recipe since it basically just consists of spreading yogurt on a whole-grain wrap and arranging some vegetables on top, but it sure is good!

I feel like I've been making my Vegan Thumbprint Cookies since the beginning of time. Of course, I haven't been—it's just that I make them so often! In fact, I always have these cookies on hand. For me, they substitute for store-bought (read: highly processed) protein bars. They're just as convenient and I can pronounce all of the ingredients. Paired with an apple and a glass of almond or cashew milk, they make my all-time-favorite afternoon snack.

PEANUT BUTTER & JELLY SMOOTHIE

INGREDIENTS:

- 1 scoop vanilla protein powder
- 1 cup frozen mixed berries
- 1 tbsp all-natural peanut butter
- 1-1/2 cups very cold water

DIRECTIONS:

Place all ingredients in blender; mix well. Makes one serving (you will *not* want to share!).

WHOLE-GRAIN WRAP VEGGIE "PIZZA"

INGREDIENTS:

- 1 whole-grain wrap
- 1/4 cup full-fat plain Greek yogurt
- 1/3 of a cucumber, sliced thinly
- 1 small tomato, sliced into wedges
- Coarsely ground salt and pepper
- Fresh or dried dill

DIRECTIONS:

Spread yogurt evenly on a whole-grain wrap. Arrange cucumber slices and tomato wedges on top and sprinkle with salt and pepper. Add dill if desired. Makes one serving. Enjoy!

VEGAN THUMBPRINT COOKIES

INGREDIENTS:

- 1/2 cup almonds
- 1/2 cup walnuts
- 1 cup old-fashioned oats
- 1 cup whole-wheat flour (or try a nongluten flour such as coconut or almond to make them gluten-free)
- 1/2 tsp salt
- 1/2 cup canola oil
- 1/2 cup pure maple syrup
- Fruit-only jam or jelly

DIRECTIONS:

Preheat oven to 350 degrees.

Measure nuts into the bowl of a food processor and grind until chopped very fine. Add oats and grind until blended. Add whole-wheat flour and salt; pulse to combine. Empty ingredients into large mixing bowl and add oil and maple syrup. Stir until all the dry ingredients are moistened. Use a 1-1/2" ice cream scoop to measure out balls of dough and place onto lined cookie sheets. Press your thumb into the center of each ball to create a well and place a 1/2 teaspoon of jam into each. Bake for 20 minutes at 350 degrees. Makes sixteen cookies.

DINNER
SALADS

❊ ◈ ❊ ◈

I don't know about you, but I grew up eating salad that consisted of iceberg lettuce, tomatoes, and those little croutons that come in a box. Having now discovered that salad can include a wide variety of lettuces—from delicate pea shoots to bold and peppery arugula—and can include lean meats, cheese, nuts, and even fruit . . . well, salad will never be the same as far as I'm concerned.

Just like my Food Blueprint is a formula for eating, my dinner salads are a systematic way to assemble a healthy dinner on the fly. They are my version of "fast food," because I typically seek inspiration from what I've already got on hand. My personal favorite of these salads came about from leftovers I had after a Sunday night dinner of grilled steaks (see Steak, Pear, and Watercress Salad).

Because the ingredients themselves are so satisfying, store-bought dressing is either scaled back or eliminated completely. Each recipe serves one very lucky healthy eater.

STEAK, PEAR, AND WATERCRESS SALAD

INGREDIENTS:

- 3 oz grass-fed, organic flank steak, trimmed
- 1 tbsp extra-virgin olive oil
- 1/4 tsp salt
- 1/8 tsp pepper
- 1 tbsp red wine vinegar
- 1/2 of a small shallot, chopped
- 1 cup watercress
- 1/4 cup red onion, thinly sliced
- 1/2 of a ripe pear, peeled and thinly sliced
- 1 tbsp reduced-fat blue cheese, crumbled

DIRECTIONS:

Season steak with salt and pepper, then grill approximately 3 to 4 minutes on each side or until desired degree of doneness. Place steak on a cutting board; let stand 5 minutes. Cut across the grain into very thin slices. Better yet, use leftover steak when you've got it on hand.

Mix the oil, salt, pepper, vinegar, and shallot in a small bowl and whisk to combine. Add the watercress to the bowl and toss with dressing.

Arrange dressed watercress on a plate. Top with onion and pear; sprinkle with cheese. Top with steak and enjoy!

SPINACH SALAD WITH STRAWBERRIES AND WALNUTS

INGREDIENTS:

- 2 cups baby spinach
- 1 cup strawberries, quartered
- 1/4 cup chopped walnuts, toasted
- 1/4 cup reduced-fat blue cheese, crumbled
- 1 tbsp light champagne salad dressing

DIRECTIONS:

Assemble all ingredients and enjoy!

PEACH, GORGONZOLA, AND PECAN SALAD

INGREDIENTS:

- 2 cups mixed baby greens
- 1 peach (or pear works well too), sliced
- 1/4 cup Gorgonzola cheese, crumbled
- 1/4 cup pecans, toasted and chopped
- 1 tbsp light champagne salad dressing

DIRECTIONS:

Assemble all ingredients and thank me later.

SPICY BLACK-BEAN BURGER SALAD

INGREDIENTS:

- 2 cups organic mixed baby greens
- 1 spicy black-bean burger (MorningStar Farms, or other brand), heated and chopped
- 1/3 cup yellow bell peppers, diced
- 1/3 cup red bell peppers, diced
- 1/3 cup orange bell peppers, diced
- 1/2 cup grape tomatoes, halved
- 1/3 of a medium avocado, diced
- 1 tbsp Briannas Chipotle Cheddar salad dressing

DIRECTIONS:

Assemble all ingredients and pretend it's Cinco de Mayo any day of the year!

CAPRESE SALAD

INGREDIENTS:

- 1 cup organic baby arugula
- 1 cup fresh basil, torn
- 1/2 cup grape tomatoes, sliced
- 1/2 cup yellow pear tomatoes, sliced
- 6 bocconcini (small mozzarella balls), halved
- 1 tsp dried oregano
- 1 tsp coarse salt
- 1 tsp cracked pepper
- 1 tbsp extra-virgin olive oil

DIRECTIONS:

Assemble all ingredients and enjoy!

GREEK SALAD

INGREDIENTS:

- 2 cups organic greens (romaine or butter lettuce work well), torn
- 1/2 cup English cucumber, diced
- 1/2 cup grape tomatoes, sliced
- 1/4 cup feta cheese, crumbled
- 10 kalamata olives, halved
- 2 tbsp Classic Hummus (see recipe in Easy Extras section)
- 2 tbsp lemon juice
- 1/2 tsp cracked pepper

DIRECTIONS:

Whisk together the hummus, lemon juice, and pepper. Assemble all ingredients, pour hummus mixture over the top, and enjoy!

ARUGULA SALAD WITH DRIED CRANBERRIES AND GOAT CHEESE

INGREDIENTS:

- 2 cups organic arugula
- 1/4 cup dried cranberries (I use Ocean Spray Reduced Sugar Craisins)
- 1/4 cup reduced-fat goat cheese, crumbled
- 1/4 cup diced celery
- 1/2 apple, cut into chunks
- 1/4 cup slivered almonds, toasted
- 2 tbsp Newman's Own Cranberry Walnut Lite Vinaigrette or Raspberry & Walnut Lite Vinaigrette

DIRECTIONS:

Assemble all ingredients and dig in!

EASY EXTRAS

* * * * * * * * * * * *

H ere are three go-to recipes that I make all the time to
make *other* recipes better.

Classic Hummus is my "desert island" food. That
is, "If you were stuck on a desert island and could only bring
one food with you, what would it be?" Mine would be hummus.
If I could sneak some baby carrots, celery, and grape tomatoes, even better! If you're not stuck on a desert island, use it in
my Greek Salad as the basis for a two-ingredient dressing that
whips up in seconds.

Pico de Gallo is a staple in my house, and even though it
takes time to cut up all those vegetables, it's a bright, color-
ful (and healthy!) way to add zip and flavor to so many other
dishes (hello, Spicy Black-Bean Soup!).

Can I just say that Strawberry Salsa makes my little heart
sing?! It's both aromatic and gorgeous, while the taste is juicy
and bright. Because it's so flavorful, it adds a lovely complexity
to simple chicken or fish dishes. I've got it on hand all spring
and summer, and shhhhhhhh . . . don't tell, but I've been known
to eat it straight out of the bowl as a stand-alone salad. Yum!

CLASSIC HUMMUS

INGREDIENTS:

- 2 – 14-oz cans low-sodium garbanzo beans, drained and rinsed
- 1/4 cup extra-virgin olive oil
- 1/2 cup tahini (sesame paste)
- 3 garlic cloves, peeled
- 1/4 cup lemon juice (about 1 lemon)
- 1 tbsp ground cumin
- 1/2 tsp coarse salt
- Dash of pepper

DIRECTIONS:

Place all ingredients in the bowl of a food processor with the blade attachment and process until smooth. If necessary, add more olive oil or lemon juice to create desired thickness. Adjust seasonings to taste. Enjoy with all the veggies your little heart desires!

PICO DE GALLO

INGREDIENTS:

- 1 small onion, diced (red is especially pretty, but white works too)
- 2 cups grape tomatoes, sliced into quarters
- 1/2 red bell pepper, diced
- 1/2 orange bell pepper, diced
- 1/2 yellow bell pepper, diced
- 1 medium jalapeño, diced
- 1/2 cup fresh cilantro, minced
- Zest and juice from 1 lime
- 1 tsp salt

DIRECTIONS:

Combine all ingredients in a large bowl and allow flavors to meld for several hours before using. Refrigerate for storage, up to 4 days.

STRAWBERRY SALSA

INGREDIENTS:

- 2 pounds strawberries, washed and quartered
- 1 pound grape tomatoes, halved
- 1/4 cup red onion, diced
- 1/4 cup cilantro, chopped
- 1/4 jalapeño, minced
- 1 clove garlic, crushed
- 1 lime, zested and juiced
- 1 tbsp olive oil

DIRECTIONS:

In a large bowl, combine all ingredients. Toss them all together to mix and coat. Cover dish and refrigerate for 2 hours to chill.

Acknowledgments

• • • • • •

Though it may be unusual to start by thanking someone other than your spouse or kids, I must first credit Amy Mohelnitzky with giving me the courage to publish my story. Amy was the facilitator at the Group Health Cooperative Family Wellness Program (in Seattle) that my son Connor and I attended together. Her warmth and humor, combined with her we've-got-this! optimism gave Connor and me the confidence that we could indeed turn around his situation. Amy and I became friends, and before long she wheedled it out of me that I'd been journaling about my own weight-loss experience for quite some time. The reason Amy goes first in the acknowledgments is simple: there would be no book if she had not assured me that all the scribbling in those journals—hundreds of pages' worth—was actually a book, and that the world needed to read it. And after reading much of that scribbling, it is Amy who came up with the book's title: *Eat Like It Matters*. (Though the subtitle's all me. Ahem.) As soon as she said it I knew that *Eat Like It Matters* was the perfect way to sum up what I'd learned through my weight-loss journey. Thanks for the insight, the courage, and the title, Amy.

After I'd converted all of that scribbling (yes, the first draft was literally written out longhand) into a Word document, it was Andrea Dunlop at Girl Friday Productions in Seattle who patiently crafted a structure for the book. Andrea spent countless hours guiding me through the labyrinth of publishing, and also through the tangle of my own disjointed writing. Early on in our relationship I remember she told me that my first manuscript—those hundreds of pages that I initially handed her—was the scaffolding on which the book would be built. Upon hearing that, I was crestfallen. *I've already written so much*, I thought. *How can this possibly not be the final book?* Ah, little did I know. And thank goodness I listened to her! Under her (mostly) gentle guidance, cohesive chapters began to emerge, and my writing became more personal and focused. And even though she assures me I am not the slowest writer she's ever known, I am so grateful for her patience as I not only wrote a book, but also overcame my fears of sharing my innermost vulnerabilities with the world.

Writing a book isn't the hardest part of publishing. The hardest part is reading the comments your editor makes about your writing. In my (admittedly limited) experience, the editor reads your manuscript, says all kinds of glowing, wonderful things about it . . . and then the hammer falls. In my case the hammer was wielded by a tremendously talented and thoughtful editor in the person of Gail Hudson. Gail is herself an author and writing coach, so perhaps that explains the kindheartedness of her suggestions and the continual reassurance she offered me throughout the editing process.

So many others offered support and expertise in the way of design and production talent. The entire team at Girl Friday Productions embraced my book from the very beginning and helped me realize my dream in print. And goodness knows this book would not be so beautiful had it not been for my friend and consummate design maven, stylist Lacie Powell (Seattle).

Long before the photo shoots and press releases, Josh Amato and Matthew Lundh of Sermo Digital (Seattle) were burning the midnight oil creating my website, producing my videos, and teaching me what in the world tweeting was all about. As anybody who's involved in publishing will tell you, there's a whole lot more to writing a book than just writing. These days an author must have an established platform—spanning every type of media—from which to launch that book. Because of Josh, Matthew, and their team, I feel like I'm standing on the 10-meter high dive at the Olympics. Great platform, guys. Thanks.

One of my team members that I write about in the book deserves special recognition: my personal trainer, Taryn Langlois (Performance Colorado, Colorado Springs). Taryn and I began working together at my local YMCA just before I had knee surgery in 2012. She trained me through that rehabilitation, helping me maintain my fitness despite my physical limitations. When she moved to Colorado a few months later we both assumed it was good-bye, though we remained in touch. I'd worked with other trainers before and knew how special Taryn was. Months later, unable to bring myself to hire another trainer, I approached Taryn about the possibility of working out together via Skype. We decided to give it a try and have been training that way ever since. I've come to appreciate that a personal trainer is so much more than an exercise coach; a good trainer is part coach, but also part doctor, part therapist, and part best girlfriend, all rolled into one. Taryn has taught me so much about fitness, but most important, she is my sounding board when I'm trying to figure out the best way to articulate a healthy-living topic. And she doesn't even skip a beat when I text her just before a workout and say, "Please don't kill me today!"

Sharing my family and childhood stories has been difficult at times, but my parents' support of my journey to health and happiness has never wavered. Though they divorced when I was still in elementary school, they have always been united in their love and support for me. As adults we tend to lay a lot of baggage at the feet of our parents, but at the end of the day it is all of those experiences—the good and the less-than-good—that make us who we are today. I am thankful for their constant, positive presence in my life, and I am so proud to be their daughter.

And having saved the best for last—my husband, Rob, my daughters, Madeleine and Katie, and my sons, Robert and Connor—the words *thank you* seem woefully inadequate. (As I write this, I'm sitting on an airplane, starting to tear up. Which is really awkward for the guy in 12B sitting next to me.) No matter my size, these five people have always loved me, even when I couldn't love myself. I am indebted to them for their patience and compassion as I struggled to find my new life, and even as I overhauled our family's diet and activities. Being Rob's wife and my children's mother is the greatest joy of my life, and I wouldn't have missed one second of it for anything in the world.

Permit me one final thank-you? It may sound odd, but there is one more acknowledgment that must be made. I'm not sure what to call it, exactly. It's not a person, though technically it resides inside of me. For lack of anything better to call it, I thank the spark that exists in me. I refer to the spark that I found at the bottom of my darkest moments. The spark that spoke to me and told me that no matter how dire my circumstances seemed, no matter how hopeless I felt, I deserved happiness. Because of that spark I set off on a journey to make myself whole. Was it the voice of God? I haven't a clue. What I *do* know is that—deep down inside—we all have that spark. We all deserve happiness, and we all have the capacity to transform ourselves. Wherever it came from, that tiny spark lit a fire in me that will burn brightly for the rest of my life. And I am eternally grateful.

About the Author

© Kate Baldwin Photography

In 2007, after being morbidly obese for decades, Marilyn McKenna began her journey into weight loss and fitness. Since then, she has lost 120 pounds and transformed herself into an athlete who runs marathons, competes in triathlons, practices yoga, and participates in a wide variety of athletic pursuits.

Marilyn received her bachelor's and master's degrees from the University of Washington. There she met Rob McKenna, to whom she has been married for more than twenty-eight years.

During her husband's career as an elected official on the King County (Seattle) Council and as Washington State's attorney general, Marilyn was a very public political spouse who was hiding a very private pain. Now, she is a passionate advocate for wellness, committed to helping others who want to transform their lives and the lives of their families through healthy eating and physical activity. She and her husband currently reside in Bellevue, Washington. They have raised four children, who of course *never* eat anything that's bad for them.

Contact Marilyn, read her blogs, check out more of her favorite recipes, and subscribe to her weekly newsletter at marilynmckenna.com.